HOW TIGER DOES IT

Put the Success Formula of a Champion into Everything You Do

BRAD KEARNS

New York Chicago San Francisco Lisbon London Madrid Mexico City
Milan New Delhi San Juan Seoul Singapore Sydney Toronto

The McGraw·Hill Companies

Library of Congress Cataloging-in-Publication Data

Kearns, Brad, 1965–
    How Tiger does it : put the success formula of a champion into everything you do /
Brad Kearns.
        p.   cm.
        ISBN 978-0-07-154564-8 (alk. paper)
        1. Golf—Psychological aspects.   2. Golfers—Psychology.   3. Golf—Training.
    4. Success.   5. Woods, Tiger.   I. Title.

    GV979.P75K43 2008
    796.352—dc22   2007039720

Material from Connell Barrett, "The Tiger Rules," *Golf Magazine*, April 2006, reprinted by
    permission.
Material from Tom Callahan, *In Search of Tiger: A Journey Through Golf with Tiger Woods*,
    New York: Three Rivers Press, 2003, reprinted by permission of the author.
Material from David Owen, *The Chosen One: Tiger Woods and the Dilemma of Greatness*,
    New York: Simon and Schuster, 2001, reprinted by permission of the author.

1 2 3 4 5 6 7 8 9 10 11 12 13 14 15 16 17 18 19 20   DOC/DOC   0 9 8

ISBN 978-0-07-154564-8
MHID   0-07-154564-6

McGraw-Hill books are available at special quantity discounts to use as premiums and
sales promotions or for use in corporate training programs. To contact a representative,
please visit the Contact Us pages at www.mhprofessional.com.

This book is printed on acid-free paper.

This book is dedicated to the person who introduced me to golf, among other things—Dr. Walter Kearns, who embodies all of Tiger Woods's peak performance attributes as a golfer and father.

CONTENTS

ACKNOWLEDGMENTS

I am grateful for the support and hard work of Farley Chase at the Waxman Literary Agency in making this project happen. Ron Martirano of McGraw-Hill displayed tremendous interest, creativity, and encouragement—from the initial brainstorming that led to this project all the way through his helpful editing of the work. Others contributed wonderfully to the end product, including McGraw-Hill production coordinator Julia Anderson Bauer in the Chicago office and master copyeditor Laura Gabler. Catherine Fisse provided extraordinary insight into and strategic feedback on the original manuscript, assisting me in communicating my ideas effectively and making sense. Brilliant insights were contributed by many, who are named throughout the text. The Google search engine came through every time, making fact checking a breeze.

Thanks to the Kearns and Dunigan families, for their support and encouragement. Ray Sidney of Big George Ventures provided great assistance during this project with private jet travel, gourmet meals, and quality affordable housing.

Thanks to Tiger Woods, for motivating and inspiring millions with his athletic skills and honorable character. With Tiger being among the most exposed and analyzed athletes in history, I benefited greatly from the work of other authors and journalists. These resources are listed in the rear of the book.

INTRODUCTION

I believe it was the greatest golf shot of all time. I might not find many experts to agree, because it wasn't struck at a major championship. However, this single shot was unrivaled in symbolic power and was hit under incredibly dramatic, unprecedented, and bizarre competitive circumstances. As you might imagine, this shot decided the winner of the tournament. Nothing special there; many weeks on the PGA Tour, the guy who wins will stick an approach close, drain a putt, or get up and down and hence lay claim to striking the "winning shot." Except this time the statement was literally true. For the first time ever in pro golf—and unlikely to ever happen again—the winner only had to hit a single shot on Sunday to win a tournament. The club was a six-iron, and the shot represented the final crushing blow against traditionalism and elitism left in the free-for-all that is today's big-time pro sports.

The setting for the shot was the January 1997 Mercedes Championships at the La Costa Resort and Spa north of San Diego, California. This season-opening tournament included only those who had won a PGA Tour event the previous year. I was there on Thursday with my golfing dad and brothers, as per our tradition over two decades. Our time-tested strategy was to enjoy front-row action midweek and then head home, beat the crowds, and watch the weekend action on TV. The headliner at this event was Tom Lehman, the world's number-one-ranked golfer, coming off a breakthrough year when he was runner-up at the U.S. Open, won the British Open comfortably after a brilliant 64 in the third round, and then took down the best of the best at the season-ending Tour Championship (two months prior to La Costa) by an incredible six strokes. He won the money title, scoring title, and player-of-the-year honors. Here, in the second week of 1997, the champ was picking up right where he had left off. Hole after hole, he fired iron shots right at the flag, methodically taking strokes off par and racing into the first-round lead with a 66.

Golf at its finest, right? Except things were strange. Only a couple dozen people were watching the world's top-ranked golfer do his thing that morning at La Costa. A few holes ahead of him, however, a young Tiger Woods—who had made a spectacular professional debut late in the previous year and was now beginning his first full season on Tour—had attracted a massive midweek gallery of perhaps three thousand people. Since Tiger had arrived on Tour late in the 1996 season, golf had been in a state of chaos. Weekly, woofing masses stormed through tournament gates (tripling previous gallery sizes), rudely shoving aside the country-club fans and their periscopes, cute folding peg-chairs, and mannerly applause. They came to see a colorful player—literally and figuratively—single-handedly take over the entire sport and integrate it into mainstream society before his class graduated from Stanford.

After two rounds, Lehman led by four shots, but Tiger stormed back on Saturday to catch him at 14-under. His performance that day on the 569-yard par-5 seventeenth hole, nicknamed the Monster by the locals (the seventeenth is situated directly into the prevailing winds that blow off the Pacific a few miles west of the course), revealed why his gallery was ten times that of his peers. Hitting a massive drive followed by an equally thunderous three-wood onto the green for a two-putt birdie, Tiger became the first golfer ever to reach the seventeenth green in two shots. As related in Charles P. Pierce's April 1997 article in *GQ*, "Tiger took a wood out of his bag. The gallery erupted. It had been a long time since any golf gallery cheered someone for removing a club from his bag. The ovation . . . was about courage and risk and athletic daring."

Tiger and Tom's 14-under left the duo five shots clear of the field, setting up an age-old showdown of champ versus newcomer for Sunday. Spoiling those plans was a storm rolling in from the nearby Pacific that deluged this low-lying course accustomed to very little rain. The players waited around for several hours, cooped up in a small lounge bursting with nervous energy. In the afternoon, officials finally declared the marsh—er, golf course—unplayable, the round cancelled, and the purse paid according to the standings at fifty-four holes. The only thing left to determine was the winner, by sudden-death play-off. Because only one hole was playable on the course (the 188-yard par-3 seventh, consisting of a tee, a pond, and a green), Woods and Lehman would play this hole, over and over again if necessary, until a winner was decided.

When the sudden-death play-off was announced, the two players headed to the practice range for an allotted warm-up period. There, another glimpse of new golf was offered to close observers. As Tiger related in an interview at a Buick promotional event in San Diego a decade later, "I knew that it was only a one hole play-off, and I saw Tom going through his whole routine like he normally would, hitting wedges, eight-irons, maybe driver, everything in the bag. I was thinking, boy, I don't know if that's quite the right game plan. We're playing one hole and one hole only. I'm going to keep hitting whatever it is. I'm going to hit six-iron and I'm going to hit seven-iron. It depends on how the wind switches."

Seems like a trivial issue—after all, a warm-up session is mainly to get the muscles loose and the timing down. Golf tradition has it that you start with short pitch shots and work your way through the bag, eventually launching bombs with the driver. With his driving-range club selection, the newcomer informed everyone that he was bulldozing tradition. In the years ahead, more tradition would be bulldozed, literally, as many courses (most notably the hallowed Augusta National, host of the Masters) would spend millions of dollars "Tigerproofing"—redesigning holes to increase course length—in an effort to neutralize Tiger's power advantage (and that of other players who followed his lead by becoming longer hitters).

Forget the foreplay of working through the bag; Tiger was going straight for the kill, wielding the same sword over and over, oblivious to the steady rain on the La Costa practice range. The golfer of the future was here, in your face: a strong, powerful athlete with an unabashed killer instinct.

The players were called to the tee, and Lehman hit first. Showing us just how difficult it is to play championship golf under pressure, he made an unsightly lunge at the ball (Lehman's distinctive move even at his best) and chunked a horrific shot that bounced off the far bank and clunked back into the pond fronting the green. Sinking quickly with the ball was his number one world ranking, lodging on the bottom of the pond, never to resurface. I'm not sure if knowing the opponent's ball is in the drink brought less or more pressure to Tiger or if he even cared when he addressed his ball with a six-iron. "I was making sure to hit the ball right of the pin, right of the pin, right of the pin," he reminisced in the 2006 Buick interview. "I aimed in between the bunkers, pulled it a little bit, wind got it . . . it ended up closer than I thought it would be." The ball nearly flew into the cup and came to rest a few inches from the hole, forming an apropos exclamation point with the flag stick. As Charles P. Pierce related in *GQ*, "The crowd . . . did not cheer. Not at first. Instead, what the crowd did was . . . sag. There was a brief, precious slice of time in which the disbelief was sharp and palpable . . . then the cheers came, and they did not stop until he reached the green." Tiger left La Costa with the champion's trophy, the $296,000 winner's check, a new Mercedes for his mom, and the PGA Tour's "understatement of the year" plaque.

After that single shot, the sport now belonged to Tiger, with the previous king violently and disgracefully deposed. (Well, it actually took two shots, Lehman's and Tiger's.) Over the next few years, money would steadily pour into golf like the rain at La Costa, making Tiger the richest athlete in the world by an ever-increasing margin. (A 2007 *Sports Illustrated* report had Tiger at $112 million in annual earnings that were increasing by 13 percent annually; number two was boxer Oscar De La Hoya at $55 million; number three was Phil Mickelson at $51 million; then several others followed in the $27 to $35 million range.) A few months after La Costa, Tiger would overpower the revered Augusta National Golf Club, making a mockery of the tradition by shooting low-iron second shots into par-5s and lapping the field by a ridiculous twelve shots. Tour players would be compelled, overnight, to become real athletes, in order to keep up with the new standard of length, power, and competitive intensity established by Tiger. Starting a few tournaments into his 1996 campaign when he surprisingly started winning, galleries became ever more colorful, erasing more tradition—an unpleasant one, in this case.

The prototype player with blond locks, loud pants, and a soft belly—something that had contributed greatly to golf having a narrow audience—was updated to an athlete of mixed race, bred on public courses, who looked like he could fit in on an NBA basketball court or NFL football field. As a consequence, Tiger would bring the sport into mainstream ESPN "SportsCenter" popularity. This has inspired an entire generation of youth to add "golfer" to their lists of dream careers alongside the other major sports and has brought broad respect to the sport across unlikely demographics ranging from NASCAR good ol' boys to suburban soccer moms to urban hip-hoppers. By the age of twenty-one, Tiger had already joined Muhammad Ali and Michael Jordan as cultural phenomena, larger than life and much larger than their own sport.

It's difficult to convey in words to a person who is not a player or fan of golf how magical and improbable it is for someone under tremendous pressure to nail a target two football fields away—although the description alone provides a powerful visual image. Regardless of whether or not you'll ever tee one up under pressure, we must all pause and appreciate what is arguably the greatest phenomenon in the history of sports and in the process wonder how Tiger does it. Certainly Tiger's incredible physical gifts, hours of daily practice, and years of experience predict great success. However, the obvious recipe ingredients and the high drama of his exploits can obscure the subtler champion qualities that we can study and implement in pursuit of our own peak performance goals.

Besides his physical skills, Tiger is the best because he is able to more intently focus on the present than can his competitors, he enjoys the process of pursuing peak performance (including both the hard work in preparation for and the intensity of tournament competition), and he has a balanced perspective toward golf and life—allowing him to absorb both defeat and victory in a healthy, productive manner that breeds more success instead of distraction or negativity.

For a competitor with an imbalanced perspective, defeat feels like falling off a cliff. For someone such as Tiger, balanced and committed to the process, defeat represents an opportunity for personal growth. You shed a few tears, dust yourself off, and hit the ground running with passion and enthusiasm for the next competition; no need to muster the will and energy to scale a cliff just to get back to where you started. On a job interview or a golf course, a balanced competitor projects an aura of confidence instead of desperation, which naturally equates to better performance and more enjoyment.

Awakening to the reality that you may be blocking your own path—that even some of your vaunted competitive strengths may actually play out to be weaknesses—can be hard to accept. We are so conditioned to equate success with pushing harder and moving faster that the suggestion to slow down and mellow out can be confusing and unappealing. But as we examine Tiger and other success stories more deeply than what's offered in their "SportsCenter" high-light clips, we can gain some powerful insights that enlighten our perspective and push us in the direction of health, happiness, and balance instead of simply victory.

Tiger's physical gifts and talents may be out of your reach, but the behavior and personality traits that make him a champion are there for the taking. In this book we will carefully analyze each of these attributes and provide detailed guidance for how to implement them in pursuit of your own peak performance goals.

AP Images/Bob Galbraith

WHY TIGER IS THE GREATEST ATHLETE OF ALL TIME

I believe there is a strong case for Tiger Woods being considered the greatest athlete of all time. Admittedly, it is a flawed debate to compare athletes in different sports or different eras, and there are some other very worthy competitors for the greatest-ever title—Michael Jordan, Lance Armstrong, Roger Federer, and Carl Lewis come to mind right away. However, certain dynamics of the Tiger dynasty surpass anything ever seen before in sports. In a word: money. No, not the $112 million he banks each year for winning tournaments, playing exhibitions in Asia and the Middle East, and pitching Swoosh apparel and golf clubs, Buicks, video games, razors, watches, and even eye surgery. It is the presence of massive financial incentives and the wide-open competition structure in golf that make an athlete such as Tiger Woods a once-in-a-lifetime, perhaps once-in-history, phenomenon.

No offense to the great champions of the old days, but the modern era is vastly more competitive than years past due to exponentially growing financial rewards. In the 1970s when Jack Nicklaus dominated the Tour, the 100th best golfer was selling insurance or golf shoes in the off-season to make ends meet. The 200th best golfer was unknown and undiscovered, probably giving lessons at some country club and longing for a different era. In 2007 the 100th ranked player on the PGA Tour earned $985,000 in prize money; the 200th made $175,000. At least five hundred professional golfers in America earned enough to focus full-time on reaching their competitive potential in tournament golf.

Consider the literal truth in the names of the most prestigious titles in golf, the U.S. and British Opens. In 2007, 8,544 players entered the U.S. Open (requirements: pay the entry fee and hold a handicap index of 1.4 or less, indicating the capability to play par golf). There were 109 U.S. Open Local Qualifying tournaments where the top few players in each (a total of 550 players) advanced to Sectional Qualifying. From the fifteen Sectional events, a total of seventy qualifiers joined the ranked Tour pros who were exempt from qualifying to form the final field of 156 entrants. After two rounds, the lowest sixty scores and anyone else within ten shots contested the final two rounds to determine the placements.

Golfers can pursue their sport for a career span that far exceeds the next closest sport, a span running at least thirty years when you consider the typical path of an elite player—from college on to the Tour for a couple decades, then transitioning to a few years' swan song on the very lucrative Champions Tour (for golfers fifty or older). Athletes even a couple hundred spots down in the rankings have the basic resources (coaching, equipment, access to facilities and competition, and a comfortable economic status produced by golf earnings) giving them an opportunity to succeed that is virtually equal to Tiger's resources at the top of the food chain.

The scope of Tiger's potential and existing challengers worldwide looks like this: six major professional golf tours around the globe plus dozens of smaller tours allow a total of approximately a thousand players to earn in excess of $40,000 annually in prize money, this author's arbitrary cutoff point to consider an athlete a full-time professional golfer.

Booby Traps

Team sports present a much more convoluted road to the top. A potential professional star in football, basketball, baseball, or hockey has to have a perfect confluence of excellent coaching and teams through his developmental years, have good luck to avoid the catastrophic injuries that are commonplace in contact sports, be recognized and given a fair chance to perform by highly subjective decision makers, and rely on cooperative and talented teammates to maximize competitive performances. Consequently, many potential elite athletes are deterred by booby traps such as injuries, team politics, poor academics at the collegiate level (a mandatory stepping stone for many sports), or poor support systems and wayward temptations at home, particularly in low socioeconomic environments.

Speaking of booby traps, consider the archetypal story of Boobie Miles, the protagonist in H. G. Bissinger's bestselling book *Friday Night Lights* (later a feature film and TV series), which chronicles the high stakes and high drama of Texas high school football. In 1988 Miles was rated one of the top prep running back prospects in the nation, but he suffered a torn anterior cruciate ligament (while defying a doctor's orders to not play because of a minor knee injury) that effectively ended his chances for a big-time college and pro career. Even the fortunate who make it to the NFL face an average career length of only three and a half years, according to the NFL Players Association. In contrast, a golfer must simply shoot a low score in tournament play to move up the competitive ranks. Simple, clear-cut, no politics, no high risk of injury, no freakish genetic strength or speed required, no teammates or coaches to potentially block the path—just seventy-two holes of tournament play offering an unobstructed opportunity to reach the top. Furthermore, golf's minimal physical demands allow players to remain competitive for decades.

Of all careers, sports offer perhaps the purest identification of the best, while golf (along with other individual, objectively measured sports, such as track and field) offers among the purest of playing fields. The competition is understandably brutal, as ascending up the ranks has massive real-life rags-to-riches consequences. PGA professional Brian Gaffney lent some insight into the challenges and opportunities of professional golf during a 2007 interview on usopen.com. Gaffney, a former minitour competitor-turned-club-pro in Rumson, New Jersey, made it through the 2007 U.S. Open Local Qualifying tournament but failed in the Sectional Qualifying tournament. "I set up a five-year plan [for competing on pro golf's minitours] and the end of 2001 was the fifth year of that," said Gaffney. "I didn't make it. That's really what it is. It's a talent thing. It's not how much money you have. You can be dirt poor—and I was—hitting balls in a field, but it's just a number that you have to shoot. If you are playing well enough to qualify for the PGA Tour and sustain a full-time lifestyle it doesn't matter what you look like or what your clubs look like. It's just a number. That's why I like [golf]. But it's also why I [failed to make the PGA Tour]. I just couldn't shoot a low enough number."

Every 138 Years

With money being the ultimate worldwide talent scout, opportunity equalizer, and lifestyle optimizer, what we should see in a lucrative sport such as golf is a parity-of-excellence condition. Here a rotating pool of players would trade titles and high rankings. The ensuing and often sudden windfall from reaching the highest level could predictably bring about temptations and distractions and/or loss of basic motivators. This would lead to a sifting and shifting of characters on the main stage. Fat cats—such as entrepreneur extraordinaire Greg Norman—would drop off the top level and spend their postprime years cashing in on corporate outings, building golf courses, traveling in private jets, and building financial empires. Up-and-comers with ideally focused lifestyles, adequate resources, superior talent, and sufficient hunger would achieve breakthroughs and sustain the aforementioned circle of life of pro athletes.

This is in fact what we do see in virtually every sport, save for the occasional aberration such as Tiger or tennis great Roger Federer. High-level sports offer a thrilling case study of free-market economics in action. The demand for elite athletes is high and supply is limited, so competition and compensation are extraordinary. All that considered, I believe Tiger's performance at the 2000 U.S. Open at Pebble Beach may rank as the greatest sporting achievement of all time—or at least the most impressive slaughter of top-flight competition. He shot 12-under par (breaking the U.S. Open scoring record by four shots) at what historically is by far the most difficult tournament in the world relative to par. His victory margin was an astonishing fifteen strokes over South Africa's Ernie Els, one of the world's elite players. This erased the previous "largest-margin-of-victory-in-a-major" record of twelve shots. The fact that this record had held for 138 years (Old Tom Morris faced *five* opponents when he set the previous record at the 1862 British Open!) puts this performance in perspective as a once-in-a-century achievement. With the continued escalation of financial incentives and popularity of golf, we may never see such a distorted victory margin again at the world's most competitive and prestigious tournament.

THE FACT THAT THIS RECORD HAD HELD FOR 138 YEARS PUTS THIS PERFORMANCE IN PERSPECTIVE AS A ONCE-IN-A-CENTURY ACHIEVEMENT.

Caffeine, Cigarettes, and Natural Talent

There has been great debate as to how much significance genetics plays in the role of creating and determining who will become a champion athlete. Dr. Max Testa, one of the cycling world's foremost sports performance physicians, offers this succinct observation: "genes determine who makes it into the pro peloton [the word for "pack" in a bicycle race], but not who wins the race." In the sports that have strong physical prerequisites, the effect of genes is blatant. The most exhaustive and fascinating work on the subject is Jon Entine's *Taboo: Why Black Athletes Dominate Sports and Why We Are Afraid to Talk About It*.

While sports sociologist Harry Edwards's powerful message cautioning us against drifting to the "blacks are closer to beasts" racist mind-set lurks in the back of everyone's mind, Entine calmly presents incredible statistics that confirm the genetic advantages playing out in modern sport. In the 100-meter dash, perhaps the most pure and simplest of all athletic events, the top 200 performers of all time, 494 of the top 500, and all 32 finalists of the last four Olympic Games, traced their ancestry to West Africa. Entine follows up with a bullet list of physical advantages possessed by West African blacks for explosive sports: relatively less subcutaneous fat on arms and legs, proportionately more lean body and muscle mass, broader shoulders, larger quadriceps, higher levels of testosterone, higher percentage of fast-twitch muscles, more anaerobic enzymes, and so forth. While Entine presents a strong case for the role of genetics and race, he takes pains to remind us that genetics merely provides a starting point advantage (or disadvantage) in relation to the average. It's up to the individual competitor to leverage whatever genetic gifts are present in order to compete at the top level.

A fair number of narrow-minded sports columnists and radio talk-show hosts like to remind us that "golf is not a sport"—I guess because no one is getting hit and physical exertion is negligible. The counterpoint of Tiger's athletic appearance and devoted workout regimen is diluted when you look at the frumpy pack of challengers that populate the leaderboards each week. At the stifling one-hundred-degree temperatures and humidity of the 2007 PGA Tournament in Tulsa, Oklahoma, John Daly eschewed water on the course ("every time I drink water during a round I make a bogey," he once told "60 Minutes"), touting a better strategy to beat the heat. "I light up a cigarette and drink some caffeine, and it actually works," he told the assembled press after lighting up the leaderboard with his first-round 67.

Clearly, PGA Tour players have less-overt athletic and physiological gifts than other athletes. In a crowded airport terminal, it would be impossible to pick out the PGA Tour player blessed with exceptional fine and gross motor skills, kinesthetic awareness, and a bulletproof competitive psyche, but these gifts are just as impressive as those of a powerful home-run hitter or basketball dunker.

STARTING WHEN HE WAS ELEVEN MONTHS OLD, TIGER DISPLAYED A SENSE OF RHYTHM AND KINESTHETIC AWARENESS THAT MADE HIM THE MOST NATURALLY TALENTED YOUNG GOLFER EVER.

When three-year-old Tiger Woods shot a 48 for nine holes on the regulation-length Navy Golf Course in Cypress, California, something special was on display. I remember reading the Southern California Junior Golf newsletter about the young prodigy and thinking it was some kind of hoax—or a crazy parent kicking the ball into the hole! Starting when he was eleven months old, when he famously grabbed a club, imitated his father Earl's swing, and whacked a perfect shot into a net in his garage, Tiger displayed a sense of rhythm and kinesthetic awareness that made him the most naturally talented young golfer ever. Prodigies in piano, mathematics, golf, or anything else have brains and bodies that are naturally suited to their endeavors.

Tiger's first teacher besides his father was former PGA Tour player Rudy Duran at the Heartwell public course in Long Beach, California. When initially approached by Earl, Duran refused to teach a child that young—until he saw Tiger hit a few shots on the range. As Howard Sounes related in *The Wicked Game*, a painstakingly researched story on the history and business of modern golf via biographies of Arnold Palmer, Jack Nicklaus, and Tiger Woods, "Tiger took out a little 2½ wood and smacked three or four perfect little shots—with a tiny bit of draw—seventy yards in the air. [Duran said,] 'He could actually hit (on) three different planes [trajectories] (with) his little seven iron the first day I saw him. . . . At four, he was like a shrunken five handicapper.'"

At Stanford, Tiger would regale teammates with trick shots on the practice range: chipping a ball straight up and into a trash barrel right in front of him or hitting a monster slice drive that took off headed straight for the student dorms and curved sharply back onto the range. He has wowed the engineers at Nike Golf with his precise awareness of technical aspects of his swing and equipment. As related in Connell Barrett's 2006 *Golf Magazine* article "The Tiger Rules," "After testing five prototype drivers, Tiger said, 'I like the heavy one best.' Huh? The Nike lab guys were certain that each club weighed exactly the same. Tests later showed that the driver Tiger preferred was in fact heavier than the rest of the batch—by a weight equivalent to two cotton balls." His thirty-second wordless Nike commercial in 1999 has become something of legend. Accomplished in only four takes, he bounces a ball on the face of his sand wedge forty-nine times—behind the back, between the legs, switching hands, stopping it cold, and restarting—then whacks it in midair down the driving range to end with a flourish.

As a young player, Tiger won Junior World (a prestigious age-division tournament in San Diego drawing top competitors from around the globe) six times, then the U.S. Junior Amateur three times and the U.S. Amateur three times in six consecutive years. This is all extraordinary, unprecedented, and unlikely to ever be equaled, but perhaps even more significant than his prodigal physical gifts and performance record is Tiger's innate enjoyment for playing and practicing golf. For a little kid to beg his dad to take him to the golf course every single day starting at age three was where Tiger rose above the many other kids who showed remarkable athletic gifts but didn't rise to the top level. "There's a perception of my father that he made me work hard, hit a bunch of golf balls," Tiger told the audience at a 2005 clinic. "Actually, it's the exact opposite. I pushed him! Every day, I'd call his work and say, 'Pop, let's go practice.' In essence, I made him a better golfer!" Tiger joked.

"IT'S THE CHILD'S DESIRE TO PLAY THAT MATTERS, NOT THE PARENT'S DESIRE TO HAVE THE CHILD PLAY."

—Tiger Woods

Overeager parents should take note of a pointed anecdote from hockey legend Wayne Gretzky, where a parent asked him, "What can I say to my kid to get him to practice more?" To which Gretzky replied, "No one ever had to tell me to practice." To be sure, coaxing, cajoling, and bribing will work through a certain age range (because kids generally want to please their parents), but there are tons of teenage slackers chilling at the mall who have graduated from such regimented programs in their earlier years. As Tiger reminds us, "It's the child's desire to play that matters, not the parent's desire to have the child play."

Fueling the Competitive Fire

While Earl was the volunteer Green Beret who famously and purposefully hazed young Tiger on the golf course—making noise during his swing and blatantly cheating in head-to-head matches in the interest of making Tiger battle resilient—it's Tida Woods who stakes claim to making Tiger emotionally tough and supercompetitive. "Old man [Earl] is soft," Tida says in Tom Callahan's revealing *In Search of Tiger*. "He cry. He forgive people. Not me. I don't forgive anybody." Callahan adds, "Tida never forgives, Tiger seldom does; neither of them ever forgets. They revel in paybacks for the rest of their enemies' lives."

Much has been made of Tiger's penchant for holding grudges, freezing people out, or eliminating them entirely from his inner circle for transgressions, keeping a tight leash on his posse and demanding the ultimate respect from peers, media, and the entire planet. Here's a quick list of some people who have "crossed" Tiger and the consequences, as related in "The Tiger Rules":

> At the 2000 President's Cup, a match play event pitting USA players against a global team, Tiger noticed the caddy of his opponent Vijay Singh wearing a hat with "Tiger Who?" embroidered on it. "I wanted him real bad," Tiger said after his 2 and 1 victory. At one point during the round, their match became inconsequential when Team USA secured a mathematical overall victory in the clubhouse. When Singh extended his hand to Tiger [in concession and congratulations for the Team USA victory, Barrett

relates], "Tiger pulled him close. 'Don't forget our match. I'm looking you in the eye.' "

Stephen Ames was asked on the practice tee the day before an infamous World Match Play match with Tiger about his prospects: "Anything can happen, especially where he's hitting the ball," a reference to Tiger's self acknowledged accuracy struggles at that time. [The next day, Tiger produced the all-time record match-play slaughter, a victory by the mathematically perfect margin of 9 and 8—nine holes ahead with only eight to play—ending the match after the absolute minimum possible ten holes of play.] Afterward, Tiger exchanged these words with the media: "Did you hear about Ames' comments?" "Yes." "Did they motivate you?" "Yes." "Care to comment further?" "Nine and 8."

Michael Campbell was asked the same before his World Match Play match with Tiger in 2000. "Hell, yes, I have a chance. I want Tiger. I'm not here to fill out the field." On the first tee Tiger stared Campbell down and whispered, "I heard you want a piece of me. Now, you've got me." Tiger birdied three of the first four holes, ended the match after 14 and sent Campbell home. "I thought I was ready to take on the world, but I wasn't. That was a very humbling experience," Campbell admitted afterward.

Tiger has famously fired people on his team for attracting excess attention or otherwise breaking a Tiger omertà of decorum and discretion. Most notable was his first pro caddie, Fluff Cowan, likely sacked for cashing in on his broadcast background fame by doing cheesy commercials and holding court on such taboo topics as his compensation ($1,000 a week plus a percentage of prize money). Tiger froze out CBS commentator Peter Kostis and former swing coach Butch Harmon for a requisite period simply for critiquing his swing. These petty disputes and grudges are seemingly not aligned with the characterization of Tiger as the evolved, balanced, Zenned-out athlete of the future. Let's remember that they only represent one facet of Tiger's success formula, although judging by history, it seems to be an essential one. Like many great competitors, the balance kicks in when Tiger leaves the golf course.

In "The Tiger Rules," Barrett relates this comment from popular golf announcer–jokester David Feherty: "There are two Tigers, the guy you see at tournaments, and the guy you see off the course. And the Tiger you see at tournaments makes [Ben] Hogan [notoriously cold competitor and all-time golfing great] look as warm and fuzzy as a puppy, in terms of his complete focus. Everything—fans, media—it's all swatted away. And I have no problem with him walking right past me on the course because I've seen the other side. The funny, easy-going guy. But something happens when he puts his spikes on. It's like watching a shark feed. To see a creature that's so evolved—there's a beauty to it. It's taken to an art form."

Tiger and Annika Sorenstam have a penchant for trading needling text messages after victories. One from Annika to Tiger read, "9-9"—sent after she won her ninth major championship in 2005, tying Tiger's major victory total at that time. After Tiger's 2005 British Open victory, he texted Annika simply, "10." Connell Barrett related a third-person account of a Tiger message on the occasion of his eleventh major title at the 2006 British Open. He was paired there on Sunday with his closest challenger, Sergio Garcia, who was clad in an impossibly garish, head-to-toe bright yellow Adidas golf outfit. Garcia's 73 sagged him to a tie for fifth place, while Tiger's 67 left him two shots clear of Chris DeMarco. While Tiger told the media that his text message to Annika was "11," rumor has it the actual message read, "I just bludgeoned Tweety Bird."

To be a guarded, petty, vindictive, self-absorbed competitor is perhaps a coping mechanism for great champions to deal with the constant pressure, attention, and expectations heaped upon them while pursuing the ultimate in human performance. Tiger's soap opera kindling call to mind similar examples from Lance Armstrong and how he continually leveraged dramatic conflict to create a fresh chip on his shoulder for each of his seven consecutive Tour de France victories—from proving to the world he could come back from cancer, then defeating top riders who missed his comeback year victory, then railing against doping allegations, then matching the record of five Tour titles, achieving a record-breaking sixth, and finally going on top with seven in a row. As Feherty is quoted in "The Tiger Rules" article, "All the greats had that talent. They use what they read, what they see on TV. It fuels them. With Tiger, it's embedded in his genetic code."

Warning: don't try this at home. The business arena requires more discretion and political correctness than high-level athletics, and there is no call for the amateur athletic enthusiast to go around staring down the competition. However, we can pull a relevant analogy for our Tuesday-night basketball league, the club's tennis ladder, a weekend golf tournament, or the quarterly sales contest. It's simply a matter of, again, balance: applying the primal, killer instinct element of peak performance within the rules of the game calling for decorum.

It might serve many of us to become more comfortable with intense competition, gathering whatever fuel we need to become the Tiger shark when appropriate, then reverting to a real-life pleasantry afterward—like Mr. Rogers removing his sweater and changing into his slippers when he gets home. There are great examples of winners in business who do exactly this. They're always there, communicating in an honest and direct manner, eager to problem solve or extend a hand to grab yours and pull you up the hill. And oh, by the way, if you cross them, they will cut off that same hand.

AP Images/Amy Sancetta

2

EVOLUTION OF THE MODEL ATHLETE
MOVING BEYOND WINNING TO A HIGHER AMBITION

Tiger is arguably the greatest winner in all of sports, yet, contrary to the prevailing mentality in competitive arenas about the proper disposition for success, he is committed to something beyond merely winning: he is committed to the pursuit of personal excellence, in the present moment, and loves the process. Consequently, Tiger's mentality, emotional disposition, self-satisfaction, and happiness transcend his ranking on the leaderboard.

Directing Competitiveness Inward for Abundant Success

Tiger has exposed his tournament competitors and the rest of us rooting him on in the gallery or on TV as flawed and superficial. We mimic Tiger's trademark fist pump and watch as he mercilessly disposes of the competition, absorbing mainly the macho and overt elements of his legacy. We revel in quotes such as the classic served up by Tiger's mother, Tida, in her endearing broken English: "Go after them, kill them. Step on their throats and don't let your opponent up. When you're finished, now it's sportsmanship."

However, behind the wizard's curtain, Tiger is viewing his competitive endeavors from a more complex perspective. Yes, the object of the game is to win, but the value and the meaning are found in the process, not in the mere holding of the trophy. Thinking about the trophy during the journey is a lethal distraction, as many of Tiger's less-evolved opponents have discovered painfully. Extending your focus outward—worrying about opponents or what the world thinks of you—is also a distraction. Tiger steps on plenty of throats, albeit inadvertently, while trying to get a good stance to hit his shots. His enlightened competitive fire focuses on the process of peak performance, and it is directed entirely inward. In contrast, the prevailing psycho-emotional disposition of the modern competitor that we have been socialized to adopt in pursuit of success is to obsess on external variables and determine our self-worth according to results.

THINKING ABOUT THE TROPHY DURING THE JOURNEY IS A LETHAL DISTRACTION.

This is a critical distinction to understand and implement from Tiger's example. Because Tiger relishes the journey and the struggle, his competitors serve to inspire and challenge him to peak performance—the "bring it on" competitive disposition. Those who are stuck in the traditional adversarial, results-obsessed competitive mentality are unknowingly set up by Tiger time and time again. Instead of preserving an inner focus, they allow themselves to become intimidated by his raucous gallery, his steely competitive presence, his shots of superior length and power, and numerous other potential "Tigermania" distracters.

"An Inordinate Amount of Pressure"

Tiger's magnificent record in match play, where opponents are most vulnerable to intimidation, speaks volumes about the psychological advantage his evolved disposition offers. In match play, there is no cumulative score; you win, lose, or tie each hole until a winner is determined. If your opponent is in trouble on a hole, you play more conservatively than normal. If your opponent hits an approach shot close to the hole, you have to be more aggressive. The standing of the match also dictates the level of risk taking. If you fall behind, you have to take more risks in an attempt to win holes.

After winning six USGA national championships in six years (all match-play format) as an amateur, Tiger holds the best cumulative record on Tour at the annual World Match Play Championships: 25–6 (after the 2007 event). He has won the tournament twice (requiring six consecutive victories at each event) and finished runner-up one year. Tiger admits that match-play format requires a more opponent-focused mind-set than stroke play and is thus more stressful. However, he leverages these dynamics to his advantage by seeing match play as an opportunity to gain a greater psychological advantage than in stroke-play format. "It's a grind. You're pretty tired by the end of it," Tiger explained after a 2007 World Match Play Championships second-round victory against Tim Clark. "In Match Play, the ebb and flow of the emotional changes that happen wear on you. In stroke play, I could care less what Tim's doing today—I'm trying to get myself in position for Sunday. Today, I'm worried about each and every shot he hits, what that does to my shots. I'm trying to put pressure on him; he's thinking about my shots. It's more of a mind game than stroke play."

It's a mind game all right, because while Tiger "worries" about Tim Clark's shots, it's a different form of worry than the one his opponents feel when playing against the number one player in the world. After the historic Ames match in 2006, Tiger offered this telling comment about his match-play mentality: "It's not physical, where you go up there and put a shoulder in somebody and take him out," Woods said. "It's about the ability to bear down and pull out quality golf shots on your own, and put an inordinate amount of pressure on your opponent. That's the only thing you can do in our sport."

Tiger's worry—how he can best put pressure on his opponent, factoring in the performances of both players being that it's a one-on-one battle—is empowering. The other worry, that felt by his many vanquished opponents, is negative and fearful in nature, not strategic. Thoughts such as "Oh, no, he made another birdie and is pulling away" or "I need to win this hole or I'm doomed" that enter the conscious or subconscious mind lead to desperate strategic decisions and a diverted focus.

Seven Down with Seven to Play

This panic mode reaction famously never, ever happens to Tiger. One of the proudest accolades Tiger has earned from peers and the media is that he's a first-rate "grinder." This is golf terminology for a run-of-the-mill player who works hard and bears down on every single shot, trying to shoot a low score. The antithesis of a grinder would be the flashy champion launching bombs and knocking down flagsticks as an expression of natural talent. Think Greg "the Great White Shark" Norman in his prime; landing on tournament grounds via his private helicopter, blitzing the field with a spectacular round, and then drinking his own label wine at dinner afterward. A grinder stays on the range till dark, pays his dues on the minitours—featuring stinky motels, long days on the road, and pitiful purses—grinding away to earn a chance to move up to the next level. With making the cut so important to marginal players (even last place gets a nice check after you make the cut; nada if you miss the cut), the term *grinding* likely originated from the reality that marginal players must focus on every single stroke, even while far out of contention, in order to make the cut and pick up a weekend paycheck.

Connell Barrett came up with a top-ten list of Tiger's champion character attributes for "The Tiger Rules"—among these, a chip on his shoulder when it comes to respect, grudges, and dealing with the public; an expectation of loyalty; a sense of humor; attention to detail; and a desire to constantly improve, pursue a higher calling with his charity work, and unplug regularly from the pressures of tournament golf—and examples of how these play out in the competitive arena. In the article, Jim Furyk, 2003 U.S. Open champion and the number-three-ranked player in the world in 2007, marveled at Tiger's grinding talents after being paired with him at the 2000 AT&T Pebble Beach National Pro-Am. There, Tiger came from seven shots behind with seven holes to play to defeat caving front-runner Matt Gogel (whose backpedal tied him with Vijay Singh) by two shots. Furyk said, "Most guys in that position aren't still trying to win the tournament, but Tiger was still thinking he had a chance. He believes he can win even when he's 10 down. He never makes a frustrated, hasty play. He always plays the correct shot. He never says, 'Shit, I'm two back!' and pulls driver and hits it anywhere. He plays the course the way it should be played."

Tiger grinds on every stroke, period—whether he's miles ahead of the field in a major, seven shots behind with seven to play, or having a rare outing where he struggles to make the cut. Like cyclist Lance Armstrong, who combined his laboratory-certified freakish physical talents (he produces less lactic acid "burn" than the next guy under the stress of intense exercise) with a training regimen that was second to none, Tiger is both the greatest natural talent the game has ever seen and one of the hardest workers.

The Forgotten Creed

Tiger's cooperative, process-oriented competitive ideals are also espoused at the beginning of the athletic continuum—in youth sports leagues. My local youth soccer organization in Auburn, California, doesn't keep score of games nor of season standings, because they want kids to focus on having fun and giving their best effort regardless of the score. This is an admirable and effective approach, particularly to mute the potential damaging influence of little league parent syndrome on teams and individuals. Unfortunately, we slowly but surely drift away from these high-minded ideals as sports get more "serious." The excitement and intoxication of winning have caused many to leave the joy of the experience in the rearview mirror in narrow-minded pursuit of the checkered flag.

This cultural distortion of values is thanks largely to the influence of money. The lofty ideals of amateurism espoused by the Olympic Creed are a difficult fit into modern life. Try spouting the creed to your boss next quarter after you miss quota:

> The most important thing in the Olympic Games is not to win but to take part, just as the most important thing in life is not the triumph but the struggle. The essential thing is not to have conquered but to have fought well.

Perils of Results Obsession

Long ago, elite amateur athletes realized that their popularity in mainstream culture generated revenue—for other people. A forced inequity such as this has a way of equalizing, thanks to the dynamics of the free market. Witness the "shamateurism" of the Olympic movement and how it's been blown wide open into full-blown professionalism over the course of the past few decades. We should rejoice that this market suppression and exploitation of athletes has met its demise (except in the NCAA, whose elite student-athletes must be content with a free education in trade for helping generate millions of dollars in revenue for their school's big-time football or basketball program). Unfortunately, there are also some pitfalls with these free-market dynamics. For athletes in our system, economic worth is determined by results, prompting many involved to equate the overall value of the experience with a dollar figure. This mentality overlooks the intangible rewards of merely pursuing peak performance, regardless of outcome.

While even a minimally enlightened competitor can embrace this concept intellectually, the quest for a Zen disposition faces a tough opponent in the form of the rat-race mentality. Young athletes are dejected when they lose 15–2, even if they are playing hard, improving their skills, getting fit, and exhibiting good teamwork. We rejoice when our team enjoys a blowout victory, even when a lopsided competition is intrinsically less meaningful than one with a worthy opponent. A results-obsessed team or individual who falls short of superficial goals will often spiral downward into negativity, panic, frustration, and other emotions that hamper effortless, automatic peak performance. Even winning is fraught with peril. A naturally talented athlete who finds easy success from youth through all the stages of development runs the risk of developing a distorted perspective from an inflated opinion of his or her abilities. This leads to blind spots, laziness, and an eventual deflating encounter with a superior opponent or level of play, not to mention good citizenship challenges in real life.

Even the most blessed who can't help but win and win some more are not immune to the pitfalls of a flawed mentality. Superficial drives leading to superficial rewards can earn you a superficial toast with superficial friends on your very substantial yacht, but when the champagne bottles are empty, the yacht returns to port, and life goes on, then what? Are you loved and respected by your employees, peers, friends, and family? Have you helped others achieve their dreams or merely climbed over them to board your yacht? To the yachtsman, or the track star with the steroid-assisted world record, the superficial rewards mean everything to his or her empty soul.

Go to Sleep, Then Thrash 'Em

On the flip side, we see many shining examples of athletes and teams who transcend the pressure of winning or losing to attain pure competitive bliss. "Underdog upsets favorite" is made possible when the favorite caves in to pressure while the underdog plays loose and fearlessly. We all have nothing to lose when we play games, but it takes a shift in consciousness to accept that. When Tiger Woods faced the most intense pressure and the biggest day of his career (arguably the most pressure that he will *ever* have faced in his career, short of playing in the fourth tournament of a Grand Slam attempt or trying to eclipse Jack Nicklaus and win his nineteenth major title someday), he was able to get to that place and play with nothing to lose—aggressively and fearlessly. The occasion was the eve of the final round of the 1997 Masters, Tiger's first major tournament as a professional. He had amassed an incredible nine-shot lead with only one round left before the launch of the global sporting phenomenon known as Tigermania.

Besides the significance to Tiger and his career, let's not forget the backstory of golf Before Tiger. Augusta National Golf Club had banned blacks from playing until Lee Elder landed an "invitation" (heaved up by the Masters Tournament committee, thanks to heat applied by a couple dozen U.S. congressmen) into the field in 1975. While many of the PGA Tour's elite courses and other private clubs across America added tokens of diversity to keep the heat off, Augusta didn't admit its first black member until 1991. The PGA of America had a deeply embarrassing "Caucasians-only" written clause in its membership bylaws until 1961. Elder returned to Augusta on that Sunday in 1997 to watch Tiger. A 2007 *Washington Post* article retold the incident: "As Woods prepared to hit his first shot, Elder could barely speak as tears flooded his eyes. '[If] Tiger Woods wins here, it might have more significance than Jackie Robinson's break into baseball. No one will turn their head when a black man walks to the first tee.'"

Burdened by the magnitude of the next day's round, Tiger was tossing and turning at midnight. Tiger noticed his dad, Earl, across the room also having trouble sleeping. Tiger told the *New York Times* in a 2007 article what his dad said to him on that occasion. "He said, 'You know what? Just go to sleep. You know it's going to be the most important round of your life, but you can handle it. Just go out there and do what you do. Just get in your own little world and go out there and thrash 'em.'"

Note the contrast between Earl's suggestion and another popular coping mechanism used by athletes facing pressure, the old "just pretend it's an ordinary competition" admonition. This probably messes up the subconscious more than anything. Regardless of any attempts to deny reality (using mantras, iPod auditory stimulation, tricky visualizations such as imagining the audience in their underwear, and so forth), your mind and your senses will become overwhelmed with evidence to the contrary on the big day. As Earl realized, better to just face the music head-on and learn to revel in it: sleep well, stay focused, and thrash the competition. Tiger has essentially preserved this disposition—aggressive, focused, in control, realistic about his position and impact on the golf and sporting world—and has embraced it completely. His ability to thrive on center stage gives him a tremendous advantage over competitors who lack his frequent experience playing in the spotlight.

Forty Million Reasons to Choke

If you are having a hard time buying the idea that it's a negative to be consumed with victory, let's examine the final round of the 2006 U.S. Open, where we saw a demonstration for the ages of the effects of pressure on the world's elite players. Padraig Harrington, a top-ten world-ranked player from Ireland, ruined a bogey-free round and a chance at the title by bogeying the final three holes to lose by two shots to eventual winner Geoff Ogilvy of Australia. Jim Furyk, the 2003 U.S. Open champion ranked number three in the world in 2007, quietly bogeyed 15 and 18 to lose by a shot. It gets worse with the last two—exhibit three being Scotsman Colin Montgomerie. Long the owner of the dreaded golf moniker "best player never to win a major," Montgomerie had five major championship runner-up finishes through the 2007 season and a stellar career as Europe's top player for more than a decade, including one of the best Ryder Cup records in history. After birdieing the seventeenth hole with a spectacular sixty-foot putt to assume a share of the lead, Montgomerie split the eighteenth fairway with his drive and had a perfect-lie six-iron shot to hit the green. All he had to do was knock it on, take a couple putts, and remove his dreaded moniker with delight. Instead, he made like a high handicapper, badly fanning his approach shot into a front-right sand trap, then hacking his way to a double-bogey-6 to lose by a shot.

Finally comes the excruciatingly painful saga of Phil Mickelson, the firmly established number two challenger to Tiger for the past few years. Mickelson, coming off a Masters title two months prior and a PGA Championship title in 2005, was one hole away from stripping Tiger of the honor of world's greatest golfer with a third consecutive major. Instead, he proceeded to engage in an improbable and devastating collapse that cost him not only the win (requiring a par) but even a play-off–forcing tie (requiring a bogey). Geoff Ogilvy of Australia chipped in for par on the seventeenth hole and then, on the eighteenth, made an excellent chip, sinking a six-foot par putt to secure the title.

With golf requiring unparalleled timing, hand-eye coordination, and emotional control, it's not surprising that choking takes place. Nowhere are athletes more vulnerable to a wayward nervous system and subconscious negative emotions that lead to errors. Napoleon Hill, author of the 1937 classic *Think and Grow Rich*, claims very plausibly that "the presence of a single negative emotion in your conscious mind is enough to destroy all your chances of constructive help from your subconscious mind," because "positive and negative emotions cannot occupy the mind at the same time." Even a tiny bit of fear, insecurity, greed, or anger arousing deep within the subconscious mind of a golfer can and will affect his shot.

When a team-sport player freezes under pressure, it's often invisible to onlookers and rarely turns the outcome of the contest. In endurance sports such as cycling or running, stressful emotions or fog on the brain are virtually irrelevant and can actually be complementary to performance. When Lance Armstrong got stressed, angry, or even greedy during the Tour de France, he would react by flooring the gas pedal and torturing the pack. In golf, emotions, physical energy, and mentality must be managed and dispersed evenly at all times. How else to hit a tiny ball to a faraway target than by moving many body parts in perfect harmony? Even worse is putting, where the actual physical effort is inconsequential compared to the ability to remain calm and focused, by yourself in the middle of a roped-off green with thousands of people watching in enforced silence.

It's not difficult to relate to choking under pressure if you've ever played any kind of competitive sport or been asked to stand up and speak in public, act in a play, or do anything else that elicits the familiar symptoms of the fight-or-flight response. Astute observers might argue that Mickelson really lost the Open back on the fifth hole that Sunday. On that par-5, he attempted a four-wood stroke from the deep rough—a risky play considering the typical club of choice for such an extraction is a wedge. The ball advanced only a foot, leading to a bogey-6. However, he is still the world's number two player and recovered quickly from his ordeal at the Open to contend for and win more titles.

I believe Tiger can be virtually immune from choking under the most tremendous external pressure faced by any athlete in history because of this: he believes that pressure—high stakes like major championships, competitors breathing down his neck, thousands of fans in the gallery—serves as a catalyst to improve his performance. Competitors stuck in real-life desires such as money, fame, and glory will occasionally or even often succumb to the pressure. The drama of Mickelson's collapse is still a distant second to the heartbreaking triple-bogey-7 on the seventy-second hole of the 1999 British Open recorded by French pro Jan Van de Velde. Van de Velde, a journeyman player with a world ranking in the hundreds, was poised to record one of the most spectacular upsets in modern times with a three-shot lead beginning the treacherous final hole at Royal Carnoustie, Scotland. Instead, he hit an off-target drive, an approach shot that clanged off the bleachers and ricocheted back into virtually unplayable unmanicured tall grass, then clunked one into a creek (for which he took a penalty drop back into the tall grass!), struggled to advance the ball into a greenside bunker, then made a clutch up-and-down triple-bogey to secure a spot in the play-off—which he lost to Scotsman Paul Lawrie. Whew!

Australian Greg Norman, by far the finest golfer in the world during his prime years from the mid-1980s to the mid-1990s, is known more for his near misses in major championships than for his victories. He's the only player to have lost play-offs in all four majors. He held the three-round lead at all four majors in 1986 (cruelly known as the Norman Slam; he won only the British Open), lost a Masters play-off when opponent Larry Mize holed a forty-five-yard pitch shot, and lost a PGA title when Bob Tway holed out from off the green on the final hole. Undaunted by these setbacks, Norman continued to contend at the highest level, racking up an amazing twenty-nine top-ten finishes in major championships and 331 weeks as the world's number-one-ranked player (second in history to Tiger, who is past 500 weeks and counting). In the twilight of his peak competitive years, Norman finally mastered the Masters in 1996—for three rounds. He blazed out of the gate Thursday with an amazing 63 and amassed a six-shot advantage heading into the final round. On Sunday he squandered all of that six-shot lead and more—with a 78. Golf fans endured this methodical dismantling of the human spirit in painstaking detail thanks to TV cameras trained on the featured duo of Norman and playing partner Nick Faldo. Faldo, his closest pursuer at the outset, went on to catch and pass Norman, winning by five shots with a brilliant 67.

It's difficult to pinpoint exactly what happens to great champions such as Norman, Mickelson, Montgomerie, Lehman, or others when their A-game deserts them at the time they need and want it most. But perhaps in that statement lies the revelation. Case in point is what Phil Mickelson said at the press conference immediately after his collapse: "I think the biggest reason why this is so disappointing is that this is a tournament that I dreamt of winning as a kid, that I spent hours practicing—I mean, countless hours practicing, dreaming of winning this tournament, came out here weeks and months in advance to get ready and had it right there in my hand, man. It was right there and I let it go. I just cannot believe I did that. I am such an idiot." Ditto for Montgomerie and his postround comments: "This is as difficult as it gets. You wonder sometimes why you put yourself through this."

After getting burned by Larry Mize in 1987, Norman—a legendary entrepreneur who has amassed a fortune estimated at $500 million and a complex guy who sometimes goes deep and philosophical but other times plays down to his flashy great white shark image—uttered a regrettable comment to the tune of, "At least I have $40 million [his personal fortune in '87] to fall back on." He also admitted that he cried on the beach at 3 A.M. after the incident and wrote in his autobiography, "Nothing could be as reverberatingly bad as when Larry Mize sank that pitch shot." Mickelson, Montgomerie, and Norman deserve points for being vulnerable and honest with the media. Their aftermath comments provide valuable insights into the emotional frailty and flawed mental disposition that sabotaged the minds and bodies of these players during the heat of the battle.

Evolving to the Balanced Champion of the Future

It's easy to relate to how the underdog's nothing-to-lose mentality can lead to a big win. Now, transplant that mentality to a heavy favorite and you have Tiger Woods on the golf course. He takes the love-of-the-battle disposition and blends it with extreme competitiveness and focus. In doing so, I believe he represents the first glimpse of the prototypical athlete of the future: one who achieves physical and philosophical balance in and out of the competitive arena.

First we must acknowledge that today's athletes are performing at an awesome standard. Thanks to the explosion of affluence and leisure time and of communication technology as well as the continuation of centuries of a strong athletic and competitive tradition by humankind, sports entertainment (for the spectator and the participant alike) is easily accessible and abundant virtually everywhere in the world.

Today's top athletes represent the most physically gifted specimens on the planet; they work extremely hard and are strongly motivated by massive fame and wealth incentives. These incentives are realized by only a tiny percentage of the very best, revealed under brutal competitive circumstances. However, today's elite athletes could also be collectively critiqued as being one-dimensional, egocentric, superficial, greedy, overly aggressive, and overly temperamental. Except for a relatively small number of more evolved athletes, today's stereotypical professional jocks are all yang—all about themselves and all about winning.

Much of this seems to arise out of necessity, due to the all-consuming nature of competing at the elite level in sport. Tim

Sheeper, a professional triathlete and coach from Menlo Park, California, has distinguished himself by remaining competitive in the pro ranks for some twenty years, despite operating a full-time coaching business. Sheeper reflects on the necessity and inevitability of a champion having a narrow mind-set: "Physical talent is similar in many athletes at the top level around the world. The mind is the only thing that sets the champion apart—the laser-like focus on winning. It's difficult to have comprehensive and global awareness when you are so inwardly focused. There is not much strength or desire to look outside oneself for anything."

Focusing on the superficial elements of competition is powerful and effective for many performers—beating an opponent, earning money, fame, and glory, or serving internal demons (such as obsessive-compulsive perfectionism, low self-esteem, or emotional scars and voids resulting from parental or peer rejection). This is true in business, too, as evidenced by the rags-to-riches workaholics who ascend to build business empires, which they usually name after themselves.

But money and winning are not end-alls. In fact, they can corrupt and stifle the process of achieving peak performance in many ways. Look at the seemingly epidemic criminal behavior among our athletic heroes, who have all the money, fame, and glory anyone could ask for but can't seem to treat society with respect. Ditto for the abundant white-collar crimes committed by business executives, where the enticement of more wealth and status is stronger than any compulsion to play by the rules. Left and right, great talents in all areas confound us by falling far short of their potential for myriad reasons and distractions, both benign and tragic, but often relating to unfulfilling goals and attitudes.

The next frontier for performance breakthroughs will not be to add on more muscles, work more hours, consume specially engineered nutritional products, nor somehow cultivate an even stronger desire to win. "The next frontier of performance could be in diverting that laser focus to gain enlightenment . . . teaching awareness, empathy, cause and effect," ponders Sheeper. The future champion must then integrate and balance this spiritual awareness effectively against the loud noise, big bucks, and bright lights of today's winning-obsessed culture.

"TIGER HAS MASTERED THE ABILITY TO BE IN THE FLOW OF THE MOMENT."

—Connell Barrett

"Tiger has mastered the ability to be in the flow of the moment," observes Connell Barrett. "I don't think he's ever heard the words in his head, 'I have to make this putt, or else'; he only thinks about how he's going to get the job done. He lusts for the opportunity to achieve success and has no fear of 'or else.' It's like he plays golf in a quiet room—all he can see is the ball, his club and the shot. He can't see or hear anybody else. David Feherty once told me how he was shocked that Tiger could walk down the fairway and be completely unaware that Elin was standing five feet away. That he could be so close to a woman who looks like that and not know she's there! It's like Tiger's in a cocoon. Most people don't have this ability. Tiger just becomes calmer and more centered, even with everyone watching him. I guarantee you that if there was a fire in a crowded theater, Tiger would be the last guy to panic. He'd start calmly leading women and children to the nearest exit. It's like he has this gene or part of his brain that nobody else has access to. This underscores the point that the mind is everything—physical talent can only take you so far."

Evolution is also occurring in the modern workplace. Google allows employees to devote 20 percent of their work time to pursue creative projects not related to their core areas of responsibility. While this policy results in a very tangible, very large expense for lost productivity, it also improves employee morale and has produced numerous innovative products that were integrated into the Google mainstream offering. Google also batters its bottom line with gestures such as serving free healthy gourmet meals all day to all employees and campus visitors (thereby promoting camaraderie, broad communication across departments and buildings, high job satisfaction, and improved employee health and energy levels) and offering other expensive perks, but the company is also obliterating competitors that have more traditional (read: stingy) workplace environments. Is Google's domination of Internet advertising revenue due to the free meals on campus? Of course not. It is, however, an excellent example of applying a big-picture mentality: Google's commitment to excellence extends beyond quarterly earnings to employee culture, and indeed the two are powerfully linked.

Tiger's unique approach offers a glimpse of and triggers the evolutionary process to create tomorrow's champion. Twenty years from now, everyone from the teenybopper prodigies at the golf and tennis academies, powerhouse college football and basketball players, and elite individual Olympic performers might spend more time away from the weight room, court, or field to pursue a broader "training" regimen. This training would painstakingly reprogram the athlete to break free of self-absorption in favor of balancing intense focus on performance with a broader perspective. The curriculum for the new athlete might include undertaking service projects in the community (to develop perspective, empathy for the less fortunate, and a greater appreciation that they can play a game for a living), pursuing diverse interests and skills (to alleviate "do-or-die" pressure from athletics and promote a more balanced life), engaging in Eastern practices such as yoga and meditation (to balance the extreme physical demands of competitive sports), and so forth.

There is some momentum in this direction already. Breeze through the pages of *Newsweek*, *Sports Illustrated*, *People*, or *Outside* in recent years and you're liable to find a 250-pound football player in the downward-facing dog yoga pose and other athletes doing off-season charity work. For those of us just trying to keep the lid on our busy lives, stepping outside our paradigm for some enlightening perspective delivers benefits in a more nebulous manner. Serving the less fortunate can help us further appreciate what we have and can put our challenges—financial and otherwise—in perspective. Mind-body activities such as yoga help calm the central nervous system, enhance the function of numerous body systems (immune, musculoskeletal, endocrine, and circulatory), and improve our ability to manage the stress of daily life. Making a purposeful effort to rebel against the manipulative forces of consumerism can help us reconnect with the simple pleasures and "important things" in life, such as health, family, friends, and nature.

Companies such as Clif Bar, Google, Patagonia, Toyota, Whole Foods, and many others have made tremendously expensive and difficult commitments to being green, simply out of respect for the planet instead of just the bottom-line driven decisions that for decades have defined corporate America (and brought great damage upon the environment). Martin Brauns, retired CEO of Interwoven, Inc., (a Silicon Valley software company lauded in 1999 by *Investor's Business Daily* for being the fastest-growing software company in the world), observes good business behavior as an obligation driven by the leaders. "I think great leaders and great human beings need to operate from an automatic, ingrained, inbred reflex to do the right thing, to be true to a personal moral code . . . a default setting that automatically dials up the chivalrous, highest road response in any situation, regardless of whether that high road is easy or convenient." These companies still have to make a profit and answer to stockholders, but by adopting a more evolved approach to competing in the free market, they are enjoying an advantage against the narrow-minded, old-school companies in the form of appreciative customers, positive publicity, and honorable brand recognition.

The fact that some green big shot can drive the high road in his Lamborghini Gallardo and sleep better at night in his nine-thousand-square-foot villa is easy to scoff at while you sweat over this month's mortgage payment. However, sometimes one must ponder which came first, the chicken or the egg. Google served free food and treated employees impeccably before they generated any revenue or equity wealth from their initial public offering in 2004. Tiger Woods practiced and played just as hard for nothing during his amateur career as he does for millions as a professional. A friend of mine researching his family tree for a high school assignment discovered an uncle who had been ostracized for some vague reason. He took the initiative to write Uncle Fred a letter and introduce himself as a nephew from the opposite coast who just wanted to say hello and start some communication without any bias. You know where this is going yet? Yep, Uncle Fred was loaded, and he was so touched by the gesture that a positive relationship formed and he ended up footing the bill for my friend's college and professional schooling.

What "It" Is

We haven't had a chance yet to see Tiger respond and recover from the devastation of giving away a major. In Norman's case, he might argue that Tway and Mize stole those majors from him, but the final-round 76s he posted on both occasions earned Norman thank-you letters from the Make-A-Wish Foundation. It's evident that Tiger would respond in a revealingly different manner. He'd certainly be emotional, but instead of crying on the beach, carrying scars around for months or years, or practicing denial by redirecting our attention to his personal fortune, he'd likely get extremely angry and then quickly move on forever.

"GET [YOUR ANGER] OUT, GET IT OVER WITH, AND BE FOCUSED AND COMMITTED FOR THE NEXT [SHOT] SO YOU CAN PUT THE BALL IN THE PROPER SPOT."

—Tiger Woods

Tom Callahan relates in *In Search of Tiger* that "Tiger has his own infantile moments on the golf course. 'You've got to be the worst golfer who ever lived!', he once yelled at himself after a botched shot. 'And you,' he added, turning to Steve Williams, 'have to be the worst caddie!'" However, he is unsurpassed at moving on almost immediately to the next shot, next round, or next tournament. When asked how he rated his anger management at a 2005 press conference for a tournament in Shesan, China, Tiger answered, "Let's just say that by the time I hit the next shot, I'm 100 percent committed to that next shot. Sometimes between the shots, I can get really hot. I'm a competitor; I know what I can do and it's frustrating when I know I didn't do it. You have to accept that and move on as fast as you possibly can so it doesn't affect you on the next shot. . . . Get it out, get it over with, and be focused and committed for the next one so you can put the ball in the proper spot." This childlike expression and then immediately letting go of emotions is light-years ahead of the self-inflicted pain and suffering that many performers, both elite and casual, traffic in.

Here's a comment Tiger made after a round at the 2002 Memorial Tournament, which ended with a three-putt double-bogey on the eighteenth hole: "I just went home and tried to cool off and get it out of my system. I didn't feel like it was best to go out and hit balls and beat my mind up anymore." Whatever his struggles on the golf course, I don't think Tiger ever wonders—as Colin Montgomerie did—"why you put yourself through this." If Tiger choked away a major, he would certainly have to go home, cool off, and get it out of his system. But based on his remarkable track record at overcoming what little adversity he has experienced in his career (for example, the slumps—or, should we say, the "Tiger Slumps"—following the two occasions when he dismantled and rebuilt his golf swing and struggled to perform at his high standard until the new swing was ingrained), he would—and has—used adversity as a catalyst to improve a certain aspect of his game or increase his resolve at future competitions. More importantly, he would walk away forever from the disappointment and not let it adversely impact his future. As Tom Callahan observes in concluding his "worst golfer ever" anecdote, "About every five minutes, Tiger seems to start life over, remembering everything that's important, forgetting everything that doesn't matter."

In fact, Tiger loses about 71 percent of the time he tees it up, while his winning percentage of 29 percent represents the most spectacular performer ever in sports. This is not Michael Jordan's 1995–96 Chicago Bulls (who finished 87–13 in the regular season and play-offs en route to the NBA Championship), a team that realistically could be expected to win every time out. We're talking about typical pro tournament fields of 132 to 156 players (World Golf Championship invitational events have about 65 and no cut) and only a single champion each week. While Tiger is always focused on winning just like Michael, he respects the reality of tournament golf and maintains an evolved, process-oriented perspective on the subject.

The difference is subtle but it's the essence of Tiger's "four shot psychological lead over the field," as TV commentator Jim Nantz said about Tiger heading into the 2007 PGA after he lapped the field by eight shots at the previous week's World Golf Championships–Bridgestone Invitational event in Ohio. Revealingly, when Tiger was asked about the validity of Nantz's proclamation, he countered with the quip, "I think we're all at even par right now [before the tournament starts]." At his 2007 PGA Championship pretournament press conference, Tiger was thrown this softball: "Can you ever be satisfied with second [referring to his runner-up finishes at the 2007 Masters and U.S. Open]? . . . Or have you gotten to the point where you can relax out there . . . off of [always] having to win?"

"No . . . the whole idea is to win," Tiger replied. "That's why you go to an event is to win. You don't go there to show up or . . . work on [your] farmer tan, [or] shed a couple of pounds. You go out to win, period. That's why I'm here, and I give it everything I have to do that. When it doesn't turn out to be the case, which in our sport is far more likely to be the case where you don't win, yeah, it's disappointing, it's frustrating, and you have to learn from it and apply it to the very next one so that you can go ahead and get it done. The whole idea is to win. That's it."

Remember when Bill Clinton uttered his classic retort to the grand jury, "It depends on what the meaning of the word *is* is"? When Tiger says, "The whole idea is to win. That's it," "it" means the journey in pursuit of the "W," as he is fond of saying, more so than the trophy. If you are bristling here that Tiger's straightforward quote is getting twisted or overanalyzed, let's admit that balance comes into play here, as well as throughout the saga. A competitor at the highest level must balance a vicious, manic, all-consuming desire to win with smelling the flowers and going with the flow along the way. Tiger and others achieve this delicate balance with aplomb; those who cannot fall short of their potential one way or another. For our purposes, a winner of flawed character or motivations is not a true winner and deep down is probably not happy or peaceful.

To Tiger, "it" is the total passion for "putting himself through this" every week and then, win or lose, moving on with passion to "the very next one." Tiger's journey is not for the faint of heart, but the rewards of understanding "it" are tremendous no matter what playing field we stand on. It's essential to accept and then overcome the reality that the joy of "it" has been systematically beaten out of you as you grow up. Little kids who sing and dance all day find themselves a few years later standing in the corner at the high school sock hop, paralyzed by fear of ridicule or rejection. A young athlete who discovers she has a special talent is often whisked away from the riffraff who play for fun, is given special treatment and attention, and is laden with expectations that inevitably permeate the blood-brain barrier and attach to her self-esteem cells. It's not as offensive or overt as the old East German sports machine (which identified the athletically inclined as early as age four and sent them to special sports schools away from home and family), but it's close. Enjoying the process of academics and education? Fuhgetaboutit. It doesn't matter if you're raising the next Picasso, Sean Penn, Richard Simmons, or West Coast Choppers motorcycle artist Jesse James, "it" means pulling a 4.0 on the straight and narrow line to utopia—a degree from a "good school"—which of course always leads to eternal bliss (hence the high tuition).

As you look back over the years at the sales pitches delivered by those trying to sell you cultural values, you can gain strength from the maturation process, steel yourself against garbage crossing your blood-brain barrier, and preserve an inward focus and satisfaction. Tiger commented in the 2006 Buick interview about how much his mental game has matured over the years. "Oh, a lot. It's just experience. I've put myself in so many different scenarios and have been successful and have failed, and I've had to learn from both. Why did I fail? Well, because of this. Why did I succeed? Well, because of this. You have to analyze, you have to be critical, and you have to understand that you have to take hard looks at yourself. Over the years I've done that, and I think that's one of the reasons why I've been able to keep progressing through the years. Trust me, it's not always easy, but my father has always harped on me, always be honest with yourself, true to yourself, look yourself in the mirror and be honest. Some days are tougher than others. When you know you've absolutely messed up, you have to admit it and move on and learn and apply. And I've done that."

"WHEN YOU KNOW YOU'VE ABSOLUTELY MESSED UP, YOU HAVE TO ADMIT IT AND MOVE ON AND LEARN AND APPLY."

—Tiger Woods

Sir Roger Bannister, famed for being the first person to run a mile in less than four minutes, was clued into the concept as well when he said, "Struggle gives meaning and richness to life. Running . . . helps us do other things better. It gives a man or woman a chance to bring out the power that might otherwise remain locked away inside. The urge to struggle lies latent in everyone. The more restricted our society and work become, the more necessary it will be to find some outlet for this craving for freedom. The human spirit is indomitable."

Bannister's profound quote—uttered way back in 1954, by the way—is validated by his stature as the ultimate amateur elite athlete. All his exploits on the track were accomplished during his time as a medical student at Oxford University. With his training typically limited to only thirty minutes a day due to his intensive studying demands, he deftly pursued his simple, pure goal: to push his body to the limit in order to achieve a growth experience. He was dismissive of ulterior motives such as money and fame and was more interested in the scientific aspects of his training, including conducting numerous laboratory performance studies on himself. He couldn't even keep the large cups he won due to the amateur rules of the day limiting value of awards; instead, he received egg-cup replicas. Bannister retired in 1955, passing on a chance for a gold medal at the 1956 Olympics, in order to devote full attention to what he considered a nobler purpose than athletics—a career in medicine.

King of the Moment

That's all fine and dandy for the British knight, but what about Tiger and his *vida loca*? Couldn't he be like the rest? All about winning trophies, pitching products, chilling on his $20 million yacht and $44.5 million waterfront estate in Jupiter, Florida, barreling ahead to become the world's first billion-dollar athlete and build an empire for his "children's children's children," as Greg Norman once said? Let's look closer. Back to the Sunday of the 1997 Masters. After a good night's sleep, Tiger played the trademark controlled, risk-management masterpiece final round that, over the next decade and through the end of the 2007 season, produced an astonishing 27–0 record when leading by more than one stroke after three rounds. In the process, he increased his nine-shot lead to a record twelve shots. You'd think that, standing on the eighteenth tee, he would be filled with satisfaction and even relief that his great performance was coming to a close; all that was left were a couple whacks and a triumphant walk, in the footsteps of the great legends before him (and also in honor of the black players who had been banned from the tournament for years, as he respectfully mentioned during his postround interview), into the thirty-thousand-seat amphitheater surrounding the eighteenth green.

Tiger's aggressive swing on the eighteenth tee produced a poor drive that hooked into the left rough. Watching on TV, I was startled to see an intense outburst of anger from Tiger. His mind was nowhere near the trophy presentation or the history books. Instead, as he had been all week, he was engrossed in the current shot and the chance to break the all-time Masters scoring record with a par on the final hole. We're thinking Tigermania, and he's thinking that he "got stuck," which is technical golf parlance for improper synchronization of the lower body and upper body during the swing, causing the hands to overmanipulate the clubhead in an attempt to counterbalance the error. He'd been working to correct the error and then—damn!—he reverted to it on the eighteenth hole at the Masters, a really important shot that he really wanted to hit right down the middle of the fairway to set up that crucial par!

Make no mistake—Tiger wants the trophies as intensely as his peers. He, too, has practiced for hours and hours and dreamed of winning the Masters and other titles since he was a boy. He's ankle deep into big boats and big houses (for years, he purportedly deposited his on-course earnings into a separate fund earmarked for construction of his dream house). However, there is an absolutely critical distinction between a results-obsessed mentality and a process-oriented mentality focused on the pursuit of peak performance. Tiger wants to hit each shot perfectly—even when he doesn't need perfection to win—and is completely engrossed in the challenge. At each step along the way toward his goals, appropriately and dramatically marked in golf by each stroke of the club, he has to release his attachment to the outcome and pursue the next shot with a clean slate and a renewed focus on enthusiasm for the process.

At a press conference two days before the 2007 Masters (where he was runner-up to Zach Johnson), Tiger—holding trophies from the previous two major championships (the 2006 British Open and PGA)—was asked if he was thinking about another Tiger slam (holding all four major titles at once but not in the same calendar year, à la the so-called Grand Slam). "No. I'm thinking about trying to place my golf ball around this course, that's about it. My whole preparation is getting the ball in play and putting the ball on the correct parts of the green and getting the speed of these things . . . and that's it." Tiger gives the gift of this perspective to all of us, over and over, and we, with the help of the superficial media, keep ignoring it in favor of pressing the issue of our results-obsessed mentality.

If you could parachute onto a golf course during a PGA Tour tournament and start following Tiger with no knowledge of the standings, you would not be able to discern whether he was leading by twelve shots or having one of his occasional outings where he struggles to make the cut, nor whether it was the final round of the Masters or the first round of the Target World Challenge, Tiger's own invitation-only event held near Los Angeles each winter. Like Sir Roger says, his human spirit is indomitable. Tiger's preshot routine, total concentration, and intense emotional reactions interspersed with calmness are always consistent.

Precious few athletes gain entry into this "king of the moment" club. I often watched the San Francisco 49ers at summer training camps in Rocklin, California, during their dynasty years of the early 1990s. One day, Hall of Fame receiver Jerry Rice participated in a noncontact passing drill. He ran a crisp pattern and caught Steve Young's pass as a couple hundred fans cheered. Then, instead of coasting to a stop, he cut sharply upfield, sprinted for another fifteen yards, and only then slowed to turn and jog back to the huddle. Rice ran his patterns at full speed on every play, whether or not a pass came. This was true on that scorching July day in the middle of training camp and for every game of his twenty-year NFL career, including his three Super Bowl victories.

I was startled during a golf broadcast, this time watching a Nationwide Tour event (the level just below the PGA Tour), that I happened upon while quickly flipping channels. What startled me were the subtle but very telling differences in the disposition of the Nationwide players in comparison to the players on the big Tour. More than one Nationwide player would, after missing a putt or hitting a shot off-target, react with visible anger and/or disappointment. These emotions were loosely regulated and easily detectable through their body language. The slumping shoulders and pained expressions after a bad shot can invade the subconscious with negativity and quickly cause a player to drift from the peak performance zone. This drift may be imperceptible at first, but eventually plenty of evidence accumulates on the scorecard.

Forget about critiquing amateur players, whose steady stream of self-limiting beliefs, negative personal commentary, and destructive behavior patterns commence without interruption from the time they pop the trunk in the parking lot until they sit down to imbibe and tally bets at the nineteenth hole. In contrast, Tiger works diligently to maintain a level emotional state throughout the round. When he does hit a poor shot, you often see him (granted, sometimes after an initial outburst) take the opportunity to assimilate his mistake in a productive manner on the spot. Usually this is represented by Tiger repeating a correct practice swing for the misplayed shot, having a discussion with his caddie, or calmly studying the view of the shot or putt for a few extra moments to create an empowering image for the next time he faces a similar shot.

Weekend warriors, take note: developing the ability to release your attachment to the outcome, give 100 percent effort on your present task, and forget about the past and the future is within anyone's reach. You can do it in your cubicle during the workday, while pursuing an education, in a friendly weekend tennis match, or, particularly, with raising children, because they are already expert at staying in the present. Of course golf is an ideal vehicle for experiencing the benefits of staying in the moment and the drawbacks of letting the mind drift to results expectations. I call it the 39/51 phenomenon. A golfer who shoots an average score of 90 (the "bogey golfer") should average 45 strokes per nine holes. Sometimes, when the psyche is unburdened and the stars aligned, a bogey golfer can come out of the gate and shoot closer to par for nine holes—getting, say, a score of 39 (three over, as most regulation courses are par-36). The 39/51 phenomenon dictates that the golfer will return to an average score of 90 by screwing up the back nine to the tune of 51 strokes.

What happens on the doorstep of a breakthrough performance is that the ego gets involved; we start to dream about the thing we want so badly. It could be another 39 for a new personal-record 78 or, for a more accomplished player, a U.S. Open title. So, instead of playing freely and confidently, the player might become too aggressive or too tentative or might express a variety of other counterproductive behavior patterns relating to fears and desires about as well as emotional attachments to a potential great outcome.

The evil twin of this dynamic is the 51/39 rule. When a player struggles from the get-go with a front-nine score of 51, the consequent disappointment can clear the mind of expectations and the body of tension. Positioned at the halfway point to forget about the score and simply enjoy the experience and the challenge of nine more holes, the player naturally acquires a superior peak performance disposition and blitzes the back nine in 39 strokes.

It's much preferred to approach competition with a clean slate—or smooth ice, in the case of 2002 Olympic figure-skating champion Sarah Hughes. Her victory in Salt Lake City over heavy favorite Michelle Kwan—one of the greatest upsets in Olympic history—was characterized by her free-spirited attitude. "I skated for pure enjoyment," Hughes, only sixteen years old at the time, said afterward. "I think a lot of people counted me out and didn't think I could do it. I didn't even think I could do it. I didn't want to skate for a gold medal. [Instead] I went out and had a great time. I said, 'this is the Olympics. I want to do the best.'" The text of the Associated Press article carries further pearls such as, "The smile on Hughes' face grew along with the crowd's din, and she nearly doubled over with joy when she finished a captivating program."

Tiger Woods, young Sarah Hughes, and others who thrive under pressure are screaming the secret right into our ears, if we are inclined to listen, express the courage to break free of the norm, and adopt a fearless new attitude toward competition. To go out and shoot 39/39 you have to let go of your attachment to the outcome and focus intently on the task at hand. Here's a July 2007 e-mail newsletter comment from Tiger, on the eve of him departing to defend his 2005 and 2006 British Open championships. "Someone reminded me that I could become only the second player to win three straight Claret Jugs [winner's perpetual trophy]. That's nice, but I'm not thinking about it. You just stay focused on what you have to do. One takes care of three."

Reference your own competitive experience, and I'm sure you can remember times when you were just happy to be there—out on the golf course with your buddies, making the varsity team, embracing a new career challenge—and you went out, unburdened with expectations or fears, and turned in spectacular performances.

The Importance of a Balanced Life and a Big-Picture Perspective

Earl and Tida Woods's insistence on a balanced approach to golf and life with Tiger pays great dividends when he faces life's challenges, both on and off the course. During a 2000 interview with *Sports Illustrated*'s popular back-page columnist Rick Reilly, Earl gave us a glimpse of where he was coming from. "Is your training of Tiger finally done?" Reilly asked. "No, the painting isn't complete. There's some more scenery that has to be filled in. Some smoothing of the rough edges. Besides, I haven't signed it yet," Earl answered. "You mean you want to see him win the British Open this week at St. Andrews, giving him the career slam at age 24, youngest in history?" Reilly followed. "Oh, no, no. That's not important at all. I mean, I'm in awe of Tiger's physical prowess and his mental strength, but his humanity and his compassion need work. They have to counterbalance his striving for superiority . . . without the proper balance, the individual becomes pompous and domineering."

Everyone can relate to the deep-seated psychological dynamics of trying to measure up to parental expectations. It's safe to assume that Tiger always knew and cared very much that he was being watched by his best friend—a no-bullshit, not easily impressed or deluded Vietnam Green Beret—to ensure his son's feet were on the ground at all times. Earl passed in 2006 at age seventy-four, but I imagine Tiger still feels like his father's watching him. For a mega-celebrity worshipped worldwide, it's an effective check and balance to have Dad pipe up that "his humanity and his compassion need work." Earl's influence could have helped improve the humanity of some other pro golfers, namely the victorious 1993 Ryder Cup team who ignominiously declined the honor of an invitation to the White House due to a consensus of conflicting political beliefs with President Clinton. The PGA brass had a little talk with them, inspiring them to respectfully pay their visit, but not before some players served up some choice quotes. Paul Azinger didn't want to shake hands with a "draft dodger"; Lee Janzen, Payne Stewart, and Corey Pavin said they were against taxing the rich to give money to "people who don't give a damn."

With Tiger taught from day one to operate on a bigger canvas than the life-or-death, dog-eat-dog mentality modeled by our out-of-balance sporting world and materialistic culture, he has been able to transcend the unimaginable pressure that suffocates the very best athletes in the world and to redirect that pressure into energy, catalyzing a higher level of performance. "Golf has been merely a vehicle for me to gain awareness for our foundation," he said in the 2006 Buick press conference. "That's what I want to be remembered for—not hitting high draws and fades, but for the people I was able to help and change in a positive way. . . . This [building the Tiger Woods Learning Center] is more important than any golf shot I will ever hit. Golf is what I do, it's not who I am."

Athletes, politicians, and other public figures are masters at saying the right thing and then acting in discord with their lofty quotes (my personal favorites are the steady slew of legislators with conservative social values who are eventually revealed as philanderers or homosexuals). However, Tiger's great efforts with youth have legitimized his quotes. In the early years of his career, he and Earl quietly conducted dozens of golf clinics to expose golf to inner-city children around the country. Seeking to impact more lives, Tiger, Earl, and the Tiger Woods Foundation principals focused their efforts on developing a permanent facility, the $25 million Tiger Woods Learning Center in Anaheim, California. The center, which opened in January 2006, serves some eight thousand kids in grades 5 through 12 with after-school educational enrichment classes. Having taken over the leadership role at the foundation in 2006, Tiger has his hand in numerous day-to-day activities.

In 2007 Tiger worked quickly with the PGA Tour to establish a brand-new Tiger-hosted event (the AT&T National, with the Tiger Woods Foundation as official charity) in Washington, D.C., with the idea of developing a Tiger Woods Learning Center on the East Coast. Besides bringing in the dough, Tiger has demonstrated a keen interest in actually touching the recipients of his charity. At the 2006 Target World Challenge press conference, he explained the importance of follow-up for role models. "You can't just be there . . . one day and give them one little bit. You've got to keep coming in there multiple times, and that's what I try and do, just keep seeing the same kids over and over again and checking up on how they are doing and . . . if they have any type of question about what road [they] should take, hopefully I can help out in some way."

Conveniently, these big-picture, balanced-life attributes translate to success in areas beyond the golf course. John Garrity's April 2007 *Sports Illustrated* feature story, "Tiger 2.0," details Tiger's grand, multifaceted life outside the ropes. In the article, Tiger is characterized as a control freak with boundless energy and a competitive spirit who effortlessly balances his charity work with the Tiger Woods Foundation, his various endorsement responsibilities, and business ventures such as golf course design.

Various people weigh in: "Tiger is a real pro in either environment [golf or business]"; "Tiger is a sponge. He has an incredible memory"; "Whatever he gets into, he gets into all the way"; "Tiger is a control freak. He wants to determine the outcome." Tiger supports the story line by saying, "I hate sitting still. I hate being stale. I've always got to be moving. I've always got to be challenged." Boatloads of money, power, energy, work ethic, and competitiveness along with a speed-dial network that includes the likes of billionaires Phil Knight (Nike founder and CEO) and Sheikh Mohammed bin Rashid al Maktoum (ruler of the United Arab Emirate of Dubai, with whom Tiger is partnering to build a golf course and residential community) will lead to big victories off the course in the decades to come. Ho-hum, no big revelations here.

What's interesting and instructive is how Tiger is able to balance the various facets of his life with incredible skill. Tiger's charitable operations and corporate endeavors are sustained at the end of the day by Tiger winning golf tournaments. His primary focus remains there, leaving him responsible for making all the other pieces fit into the puzzle. At a 2004 Masters press conference, he elaborated on the subject. "My dad always tried to tell me, there's more to life than golf. . . . You have to have balance in your life, and once you obtain balance, you'll find that life is just so much better . . . Golf is what I do for a living. I love it. I love to compete. But it does not define me as a person. [That ideal has] been something I've always tried to do when I've come up as a little boy playing the game of golf. But it's always been so hard to [not become consumed by golf]. You've got to have the right people around you, have some great friends, some great family. Now with Elin in my life, it just made it that much better. . . . I still work my butt off, but it's one of those things where you've got to have balance and that's the only way you can survive over the long haul."

While Tiger's jet-set life may have little in common with our lives—consisting of balancing our divergent interests of a nine-to-five, keeping the family happy, fed, and off to soccer practice on time, getting in shape, lowering our handicaps, and finishing that backyard landscaping project—we can take great inspiration and insights from Tiger's high-profile example and plug them into our own endeavors.

BREAKING FREE

You'll require a new bag of tricks to break free from the traditional competitive disposition and adopt a new, empowering Tiger-like approach to your peak performance goals. The following three chapters will detail practical steps you can take to embody three different success factors that I believe represent the best of Tiger and the most relevant attributes to implement in pursuit of your own goals. Briefly, the three success factors are:

1. **Focus.** Through diligent mental practice, Tiger is able to remain focused on personal peak performance in the present moment and tune out overwhelming external stimuli. The compelling goal of

hitting each shot perfectly transcends the pitfalls of fixating on winning and other superficial goals. He creates the ideal peak performance environment to excel and leverages his focusing skills on the golf course to all other areas of his life.

2. **Work-play ethic.** While a strong work ethic is an esteemed attribute for all great champions, it's not enough anymore. Merely putting in the work without enjoying the process can weaken the resolve of a competitor and bring negativity into the equation. Tiger approaches golf with the youthful innocence of a child at play, loving every aspect of the preparation and competition. Consequently, even failures and frustrations are empowering, because he welcomes a new challenge every day.

3. **Balanced approach.** Tiger represents the first glimpse of the evolution to the champion athlete of the future. He transcends the incomplete model of today's prototype performer, who is overly focused on the physical dimension, self-centered, and obsessed with winning. Tiger's commitment to being a good person allows him to access a more powerful and resilient source of motivation than a one-dimensional competitor. In times of extreme pressure, he is able to avoid the human frailties that hinder performance and leverage pressure situations to his advantage.

Photo courtesy of Brad Kearns

3

TIGER SUCCESS FACTOR 1
FOCUS

Let's take a great leap and proceed on the assumption that you are operating with a clean slate; your attempts to focus on peak performance are not burdened by self-defeating thoughts or an obsession with results. With nothing to worry about, your mind can focus on the present task with ease.

We're all familiar with that exalted state of effortless peak performance affectionately known as the zone. Sports psychologist James Loehr calls it the Ideal Performance State, described in his book *Stress for Success* as "physically relaxed, mentally calm, fearless, energized, positive, happy, effortless, automatic, confident," and so on. Japanese Zen tradition calls it *satori*, a state of natural harmony of body, mind, and emotions. Numerous sports psychology and mental training coaches mention the four Cs of peak performance: concentration, composure, confidence, and commitment. Sounds intriguing and powerful, but when you are done with your term paper on the subject and return your library books, it might occur to you that many great champions who embody these Cs in competition do so naturally and effortlessly; they would probably get a C in a class about the four Cs. Tiger reflected after round two of the 2007 Tour Championship, where he blitzed the front nine in twenty-eight strokes (that's five birdies, an eagle, and three pars—

his all-time lowest nine-hole score; he finished the round with a 63). "I don't know if it's a zone or not. I just felt that the rhythm was good. The pace was good. . . . I was hitting good shots throughout the stretch. It was nice. . . . I didn't know I shot 28 until I got to the scoring tent [after the round], until we added it up. You just play shot for shot. You place the golf ball and you don't worry about anything else."

Giving Yourself a Fair Chance to Enter the Zone

The zone is an incredibly enjoyable place to be but a highly elusive and mysterious place to get to, which can make the whole concept rather frustrating at times. Despite our best intentions, it's easy to lose control of our focus, emotions, and attitude in competitive situations. In a blink, we can travel out of the peak performance zone and into a danger zone of negativity, fear, and inhibited performance. Nowhere is this more evident—and painful—than on the golf course. Anyone who has experienced the juxtaposition from the driving range to an important competitive shot can attest to this. On the range or the practice green, it's easy to summon the concentration, composure, confidence, and commitment to execute the desired shot. But, as Ted Knight's legendary *Caddyshack* character Judge Smails demonstrated, when stakes escalate ("A hundred bucks says you slice it in the woods," shouted Rodney Dangerfield's obnoxious character Al Czervik to Smails just as Smails addressed the ball on the first tee at Bushwood Country Club), the slice into the woods manifests just as naturally as the flush shots on the driving range when no one is watching.

Why does this happen—to Judge Smails, to millions of weekend warriors, or even to the world's greatest golfers with a tournament on the line? How does Tiger remain bulletproof while facing exponentially greater pressure than even his PGA Tour peers? How can we embody the peak performance traits of a champion under pressure? There is no simple solution, but there is hope. It starts with having a desire and a commitment to get better. Basic, yes, but in reality many competitors have conflicting commitments and are not truly open to change and improvement. Instead, we create and maintain a litany of excuses, rationalizations, destructive behavior patterns, and self-limiting beliefs that ensure we don't have to endure anything risky or uncomfortable.

The late Mark McCormack, founder of the global sports marketing powerhouse International Management Group (IMG), which has represented Tiger throughout his career, wrote in his book *What They Don't Teach You at Harvard Business School* that the golf course was his favored venue for character revelations, saying, "You can tell more about how a person will react in a business situation from one round of golf than in a hundred hours of meetings." Out on the course, insights flow freely for many reasons: because of the frustrating nature of the game and the fact that athletic competition magnifies the lessons of success and failure and our reaction to them and also because the course represents a vulnerable fish-out-of-water arena for interaction with business associates. Clear personality insights and business-arena behavior predictions are evident from golf partners who engage in negative self-talk, are surreptitious about their competitive intensity, cheat on the scorecard, and so forth. Someone who hates cold-calling, public speaking, or sand traps will manifest these beliefs into unfavorable results when they pick up the phone, step up onstage, or address the ball in the sand.

Consider your commentary on the golf course or at work and where your statements land on the continuum that has accepting personal responsibility on one end and complete delusion on the other. A golfer's explanation that he doesn't have time to practice or can't afford lessons rings hollow during his five-hour rounds on pricey courses and endless purchases of expensive new clubs. Many like to blame their equipment, the weather, course conditions, or the slow group ahead before considering human error. Others are not open to constructive feedback, preferring to remain set in their ways, righteous, and in denial: "Seriously, I play better when I don't practice." Most damning are the self-limiting characterizations, such as "I often choke on short putts" or "I hate water holes/sand traps/blind shots/breaking putts." Imagine implementing actress Katharine Hepburn's suggestion to "never complain or explain" for a single golf round of eighteen holes. Could you even pull it off? What would the predicted impact be? How could the experience translate to every waking moment of your life?

It's critical to destroy and reframe your self-limiting beliefs and behavior patterns into ones that are positive, empowering, and realistic. "Realistic" distinguishes this suggestion from campy self-help advice to "visualize success" and have your dreams come true. You can step into a sand trap and visualize a fluffy shot, loaded with Tour backspin, cozying up next to the stick, but if you haven't practiced trap shots in ages, the visualization isn't going to help much. Instead, you could step into the trap with a positive attitude and realistic expectations. If you are a mid-to-high handicapper, you might accept that your odds of extrication onto the green are only fifty-fifty. Hence, instead of dreaming about hitting it stiff, you could concentrate on a realistic goal of landing the ball anywhere on the green. You could narrow your focus even more with a swing thought such as "steady legs, swing along footline, hit sand one inch behind the ball—legs, footline, one inch."

Now you are concentrating on a positive, realistic goal. Next you must release your attachment to the outcome. A double-digit handicapper thinking, "I need to get this close to save par," will introduce tension and anxiety to the beach party—lethal elements to the golf swing. Focus entirely on the process—legs, footline, one inch—and let the result happen naturally.

Ready to Win Every Time

When Tiger steps onto the first tee to begin his round, much work has already been done to help him focus for hours at a time. First and foremost, he competes only when he is ready, carefully choosing tournaments that align with his highest goals of peaking for major championships and being ready to win whenever he enters. In contrast, many of Tiger's peers are playing primarily for money. Hence, they play when fighting injuries, fatigue, and malaise, knowing that even a subpar effort will result in a nice paycheck. As Tour pro Justin Leonard said when asked how he felt about Tiger's competitiveness, "It's nice to have someone out here whose sole goal is not to place third on the money list."

Golfers, as well as competitors in other arenas who are all about money, often get fat wallets but compromise their ability to do something extraordinary with their careers. The stacks of big checks represent incredible talent and achievement but nevertheless mediocrity in relation to their ultimate potential. Butch Harmon once said that nobody prepares harder for major championships than Phil Mickelson, except maybe Tiger. The two best players in the world prepare harder than their lower-ranked rivals? Shouldn't the guys who've never won a major, whose entire careers would be elevated to another level with a single major victory, be preparing the hardest (with pretournament recon missions and specialized practice sessions to address the particular challenges of a tournament course)?

On the PGA Tour, marginal players (the grinders), fighting to maintain their tenuous playing privileges, are famous for teeing it up nearly every week, because only the top 126 money winners are assured of even being able to enter Tour events the following year (they've earned exempt status). Other clusters of players also enjoy exempt status. Among these are foreign players who have a high world ranking or past champions of major events. These players collectively fill up the tournament entries each week. In 2006 the grinder all-star team looked like this: Mark Brooks played in thirty-six Tour events; Todd Fisher played in thirty-five; Patrick Sheehan, Dean Wilson, and Shane Bertsch played in thirty-four; Brett Quigley, Daniel Chopra, Ted Purdy, D. J. Trahan, Jeff Brehaut, Arjun Atwal, Wes Short, and Steve Flesch played in thirty-three. . . . Are you saying, "Who?" yet? Then you get my point. A poor season outside the top 126 money winners (*poor* being a questionable choice of words, because even number 150 on the money list earned a half a million dollars in 2007) will relegate a player to the dreaded Q School. This is the nickname, memorialized by John Feinstein's book of the same name, for the annual PGA Tour Qualifying Tournament. Like the U.S. Open, players contest a certain number of preliminary events (based on season performance or ranking) to reach the Q School finals.

Many claim that this marathon six-round tournament is the most pressurized tournament on the planet, because the real-life economic consequences are so extreme. The top thirty finishers in Q School finals make it to the PGA Tour. They're lavished with six-figure equipment and apparel contracts (sometimes right after the final Q School putt, in the case of amateurs) to compete for multi-million-dollar purses each week. Fall short by even a stroke, and a player will have to tee it up at the Podunk Opens of the Nationwide or Hooters tours and camp in a van down by the river. As Feinstein describes the rift, "It is being shocked by how much it costs to refuel your car [from lengthy road trips] versus how much it costs to refuel your plane. It is 423 shots instead of 422 [the actual cutoff point for the top thirty in the tournament one year]."

What these grinders might be forgetting is the fact that a single high placing in a Tour event can make an entire season, due to the top-heavy purses. PGA Tour veteran Dave Berganio of Granada Hills, California, made a quarter of his lifetime PGA Tour earnings, stretching over a decade of competition, in a single weekend in Palm Springs in 2002. There he earned a cool $432,000 for finishing second to Phil Mickelson in a play-off at the Bob Hope Chrysler Classic. Furthermore, it would not be preposterous for any player fighting for his Tour card (designating exempt status) to consider any single event he enters a major championship worth focusing on and peaking for, à la Tiger and Phil at the four annual majors. It would not be out of line to suggest that if you miss two or three cuts in a row (commonplace for any player ranked outside the top fifty), it might be best to go home and spend some time on the range before jetting to the next tournament. Instead, with a misdirected focus on results, grinders tee it up every week and grind away, light-years away in approach and in results from the focus and commitment toward "being ready to win every time I tee it up" of Tiger Woods.

Admittedly, there is nothing you can do in practice to approximate tournament conditions to make you battle tough. It's just that you must recognize a fine line and mix competition with adequate downtime and preparation time. This balance allows you to absorb and benefit from competitive experiences and return to the battle stronger. Making dozens of three footers on the practice green is no substitute for making one on the course under pressure. However, if you miss a putt under pressure in a tournament, you best go home and make dozens on the practice green. In today's hectic workplace, it's a challenge to just keep the in-box clear, but it's essential to recognize the importance of being proactive and preparing intently for competition with such things as employee team-building retreats, continuing education courses, software and operations training, and role-playing for salespeople. This is particularly true in management positions, where your productivity can multiply through your team. Kevin Hayden, a forward-thinking boss of mine at Interwoven, Inc., once shared this insight during a staff meeting: "Remember, as your manager, I work for you more than vice versa. My job is to make you better, so be sure to communicate when you need help."

The Importance of Preparation and Routine

After you've taken the practical steps to pursue the proper competitive goals and adopted a healthy, process-oriented mind-set toward competition, the second step is to create an optimum peak performance environment for each of your goals and daily life responsibilities. Because these are so numerous, you must establish clear and strict boundaries between them and transition from one to the other skillfully, as we will discuss in Chapter 4 while exploring the work-play ethic.

When a healthy, motivated Tiger appears at the course to begin a round, he has made a methodical transition from normal life to total focus on golf. Prior to arriving at the course, he's eaten a nutritious breakfast, exercised, stretched, and dressed for battle. Before he tees off, he warms up for about an hour on the driving range and practice green. "You can see Mr. Woods settle into his preferred mental state on the practice range," wrote John Paul Newport in a September 2007 *Wall Street Journal* article about Tiger's mental attributes titled "Why Tiger Is Different." Describing his work-through-the-bag routine on the range, Newport observed, "Frequently, however, he pauses for a full minute or two, sometimes longer, and just stands there looking around and chatting easily with his caddie. . . . On the putting green, as his tee time approaches, he wanders off by himself and rolls two balls back and forth, walking between the putts with extreme, exaggerated slowness . . ."

Tiger's practice range warm-up concludes with a few shots identical to what he plans to hit on the first tee. He takes it all the way from pulling the club out of the bag, stepping up to the tee, and taking the stroke with his club and swing of choice. If he hits a bad shot, he repeats the entire sequence. This seemingly lowbrow superstitious routine actually trains his nervous system to feel comfortable on the first tee, a place where nerves can cripple even an accomplished golfer. Admitting to feeling nerves on the first tee, Tiger told attendees at a 2005 clinic, "I just have to repeat what I did a few minutes ago on the range"—and knowing that brings him comfort as he steps up to begin a round.

Tiger's caddie Steve Williams is also impeccably prepared and totally focused on their common goal. Even on a clear day, Williams packs an umbrella and rain gear in Tiger's bag, because you never know—and it's better to be prepared, even if it means lugging around some extra weight. Tiger and Steve have researched and previewed in practice rounds the particulars of each hole, including topographical highlights, hazards, optimum targets, and extensive details on yardage, so they are both certain of the strategy, club selection, and desired outcome of each shot. Tournament organizers help out by roping off the course to prevent the gallery from interfering with his shots and procession through the course. Overall, Tiger has skillfully placed himself in the zone, and nothing that happens in the outside world—particularly the performances of others—will remove him from the zone. As David Owen said in his 2006 article "Inside the Lair" for *Men's Vogue*, "Woods's concentration often seems to be made of the same stuff as the liquid-metal cyborg in *Terminator 2*: If you break it, it re-forms."

When it's time to hit a shot, Tiger and the rest of the pros go through a deliberate preshot routine—a scripted series of actions designed to facilitate good decision making, focus the nervous system on the task at hand, and prepare the physical body for the shot. Each shot Tiger hits is preceded by an identical sequence: pull chosen club, visualize the shot viewing his target from behind the ball, take a few gentle practice swings, then and only then address the ball for the shot. Tiger also has a refined postshot routine—assimilating the information from the shot and perhaps taking another practice swing to reprogram the nervous system if the shot was mishit. As he walks from shot to shot or to the next hole, his pace is always the same. Yes, he gets pumped up by birdies and angry about bogeys, but he doesn't let either affect or alter his routine. "There's a tendency, under pressure, for time and motion to speed up. Clearly, Mr. Woods wants none of that," opined Newport in "Why Tiger Is Different." After the eighteenth hole is done, another methodical routine commences. Typically, Tiger will hit shots on the range and/or practice putts that address weaknesses that arose during the round.

It's not easy to control actions and emotions in the heat of battle, but that kind of control is vitally important to maintaining focus. Australian up-and-comer Aaron Baddeley was paired with Tiger in the final group of the 2007 U.S. Open. Baddeley, leading after three days of masterful play, skied to an 80 on the final day, highlighted by a crushing triple-bogey on the first hole. Baddeley commented on what he learned playing with Tiger: "I saw how he never putts until he's really ready. That's something I need to work on."

Does your workday offer a parallel example? Have you warmed up for your performance with some exercise, a healthy breakfast, and some family or personal time? Do you have a figurative umbrella and rain gear handy? Or is it easier to pack an excuse into your briefcase, for use in case anything unexpected arises? Have you completed a mental transition so you can focus on work at the office? Or are you like the tormented surfer who dreams about sex while catching waves and dreams about waves while having sex? Have you roped off your workspace to keep the gallery at a distance? Or do people drift in and out with "autograph requests"—questions and idle chitchat?

If you fixate on the dramatic differences between your little world and the grand stage on which Tiger Woods plies his trade, it's easy to dismiss inspiration and guidance with complaining, excuses, rationalization, and self-limiting beliefs. Of course, your workspace doesn't measure up to Tiger's or to that of the leading salesman in the office, because [fill in the blank]. In truth, you and Tiger and I are not much different. If you take away the thousands of fans and TV cameras, you have a guy playing his heart out trying to shoot the lowest score possible for eighteen holes, just like millions of other players every weekend. The anonymous receptionist, billionaire business tycoon, and world-renowned brain surgeon all must focus on the highest expression of their talents, manage time effectively, and balance stress and rest in a busy, hectic modern life.

Will It Never End? Looking Past the Money for Motivation

The instant Tiger turned pro, he signed contracts, with Nike and Titleist, that would pay him $60 million over five years—he was set for life before he even hit his first shot as a PGA professional. Some players and media voiced the questionable opinion: "No wonder he did so well right away—Nike took all the pressure off." The reasoning might sound plausible, but it's a load of crap. What the $60 million actually represented was the most tremendous pressure ever heaped upon a rookie pro. His sponsors were not paying based on his amateur exploits; they were paying on the expectation—make that mandate—of professional success in the very near future. Nor was Tiger allowed to use the money to buy any mulligans on the course, like vowels on "Wheel of Fortune." It was Tiger who chose to make his situation positive and empowering, by paradoxically ignoring the money and focusing on golf. He also did this on the flip side when, during his amateur career, his parents amassed massive debts financing his extensive travel to junior tournaments.

In Gary Smith's December 1996 *Sports Illustrated* article "The Chosen One," he relates how nonplussed Tiger was upon hearing the news that he was an instant multimillionaire. When agent Hughes Norton revealed enthusiastically that the Nike deal—$40 million for five years—was triple the existing top endorsement contract (Greg Norman's $2.5 million per year deal with Reebok) and more than even Michael Jordan received in base salary from Nike, he was met with silence, followed by a mild "guess that's pretty amazing," Norton recalled with exasperation in "The Chosen One."

Most revealing is the postscript from Smith: "On the Monday morning after his first pro tournament, a week after the two megadeals, Tiger scans the tiny print on the sports page under Milwaukee Open money earnings and finds his name. Tiger Woods: $2,544. 'That's my money,' he exclaims. 'I earned this!'"

Tiger could have easily gone in another direction and allowed the instant money and celebrity status to compromise his performance. Studies suggest that lottery winners suffer from increased stress levels and reduced quality of life—from quitting fulfilling jobs, leaving friends behind in relocating to more affluent areas, becoming a mooch target for family and friends, and generally getting trapped in the bottomless, loveless whirlpool known as consumerism. The Dalai Lama observes in *The Art of Happiness* that, "no matter how much [money] we make, we tend to be dissatisfied with our income if our neighbor is making more."

Witness the troubling case of Hawaiian teenage sensation Michelle Wie, who played in the men's PGA Tour Sony Open in Hawaii at age fourteen and fired a 68 in the second round. While she quickly outgrew amateur competition (literally and figuratively, as she stands 6'1" and hits towering three-hundred-yard drives), Nike and others lavished her with contracts worth $10 million per year, and she turned pro at age fifteen. The result has been a highly publicized and criticized struggle on and off the course. Pundits say her too-much, too-soon career curve has stolen away her childhood and heaped excessive pressure on her at an age when she should be worrying about grades and guys. Instead, she is immersed in global advertising campaigns and taking heat from women and men alike for trying her luck at numerous events on the PGA Tour with mixed results and enduring a sensational slump that finds her far less than competitive on the women's tour than she was when she dabbled in LPGA events before turning pro.

If you want to follow Tiger's example, you have to do everything you can to create and control an ideal peak performance environment. You might not have gallery ropes up for your golf rounds and your cubicle might bear little resemblance to the CEO's grand, secretary-buffered office, but you can apply the same techniques the big shots use for your personal situation. Be your own secretary and carefully screen your calls ("Hi, how are you? I'm in the middle of something. Can we talk after 3 P.M.?"). Tell your golf buddies you prefer to drive to the course alone, so you can practice for an hour before your round. You won't shoot 69 like a pro, but your warm-up might help you shoot 96 instead of your usual triple-digit masterpiece. After cursing your ball's flight into the sand trap, you can make like a cyborg, reform your concentration and your attitude, and relish the unique challenge your next shot presents.

Stringing up the gallery ropes includes making tough decisions to deal with unproductive or dysfunctional relationships. Tiger eased his own father out of the picture when the time was right to transition his escalating business affairs to IMG. By all accounts, Earl was cool with it because he saw the big picture just as Tiger did. In *In Search of Tiger*, Earl related, "Tiger's in charge of his own life. . . . I'm the one who set up Tiger's financial empire. . . . But I wasn't even there when he signed the contract with Nike [by his own comfortable choice, giving Tiger space to celebrate the occasion on his own]. Tiger came to my [hotel] room afterward and said, 'I need three hundred dollars, Dad.' 'What for?' 'For entry fee into the tournament [the Greater Milwaukee Open, site of his pro debut in 1996].' I said something like, 'Will it never end?' but we both laughed." Over the years, Tiger has also fired Hughes Norton, the agent who made him the richest athlete on earth; Fluff Cowan, the caddie who carried the bag for his earth-shattering debut in 1996 and breakthrough Masters victory in 1997; and Butch Harmon, the swing coach who helped him attain the greatest performance level in the history of the sport, including the Tiger Slam of holding all four major championship titles at the same time. He made these highly publicized and highly controversial moves in the interest of peak performance, continued personal and career progress, peace of mind, and a happy life.

"A Master Class in Insipidness": Developing Your Optimum Personal Style

Tiger has absorbed much public heat for his perceived ruthlessness, abrupt public personality, and bland interview quotes. Search the transcripts of tournament press conferences over the years, and you will find an abundance of clichés and empty rhetoric, delivered from a thoughtful, intelligent, well-educated man with a great sense of humor. "Tiger speaks beautifully, but when you go back and see what you've got, he never really says anything," says Ken Bowden, longtime golf writer and coauthor of eleven books with Jack Nicklaus. Matthew Syed of the *London Times* offers a less charitable comment: "[Tiger's] press conferences are a master class in insipidness that drain the soul." To be fair, Tiger has also been extremely thoughtful and forthcoming at other times, invariably away from the competitive distraction—and ridiculous lines of questioning—found at tournament press conferences.

Why would Tiger launch into robot mode when he's in front of the media? By contrast, Phil Mickelson is a superstar with the media and general public. Watch a Phil interview, and you get eloquent, impeccably polite, and deeply revealing commentary about his mind-set, emotions, and performances. After a good round or bad, Phil's there signing autographs until everyone is satisfied. At home, he regularly dips into one of three fifty-gallon drums full of autograph requests he reportedly keeps in his living room.

It's obvious that the vanilla Tiger persona is a coping mechanism to retain his focus, energy, and personal time and space—no doubt modeling his buddy Michael Jordan. Unfortunately for all of us, Tiger's retreat into his shell was no doubt hastened by Charles P. Pierce's infamous *GQ* article from April 1997 titled "The Man,

Amen." In it, Pierce haughtily filled the pages with a bizarre mix of threads, including a "Tiger is the Messiah" recurring theme, and related Tiger's raunchy, racially offensive jokes (told, Tiger revealed later, on the assumption that they were off the record) repeatedly against the messiah theme. Clever, if overwritten, prose, but so opportunist as to be disrespectful of Tiger's juvenile candor and innocence. Indeed, the young Tiger in the headlights was showered with criticism from those in the audience more tightly wound than the old-time golf balls.

"TIGER IS ONLY AS SELF-CENTERED AND SELF-ABSORBED AS THE GREATEST ATHLETES HAVE ALMOST ALWAYS BEEN."

—Tom Callahan

Tiger is also not acclaimed for being chatty on the golf course and keeps his distance in general from most of his PGA Tour peers. Instead, he favors hanging out with a small inner circle of friends who predate his megacelebrity. Tom Callahan quotes an anonymous source in *In Search of Tiger*: "One veteran Tiger watcher, who likes Woods enough to say his good features swamp his flaws, nonetheless theorizes that Tiger holds onto those flaws as purposefully as he does a golf club. 'He doesn't want to change anything, because he feels it's all part of the perfect combination of what it takes to be who he is. If he got rid of his meanness, his pettiness, his cheapness, it would be like, 'Well, maybe I'll lose something then.'" Callahan gives him a bye here, too: "Tiger is only as self-centered and self-absorbed as the greatest athletes have almost always been. If Woods has a little extra vinegar, perhaps it's understandable. When one starts off as such a rank outsider in such an elitist environment, some residue of vindictiveness may be unavoidable at the top. Just a touch of a mean streak may be par for the course."

Awash in all the bright colors of golf—most notably green for the lush fairways and piles of cash that the Tour is swimming in—we shouldn't forget how the forefathers of American professional golf fought tooth and nail to keep the sport ghost white. Clifford Roberts, who, along with golf legend Bobby Jones, created the Augusta National venue and Masters Tournament that hosted the launch of Tigermania, was an avowed racist. In *The Wicked Game*, Howard Sounes relates the content of a speech Roberts gave at Columbia University: "He considered whites to be superior to people of color. Blacks were second best [after all, they did such a great job cooking and caddying for the white members and players at Augusta for decades!] in his racial hierarchy. And he had total disdain for people of mixed race. The children from mixed marriages were, he asserted, 'worthless . . . in every respect.' "

While there are varying opinions of just how much racism has affected Tiger, he has clearly been a fish out of water in his golf world since the age of three. You'd think his astonishing 48 for nine holes on the Navy Golf Course in Cypress at that age would have earned him carte blanche privileges at the facility. Instead, he was banned from the course on account of being below the age limit and then was subjected to several later slights during many of his developmental years that he played there. Earl Woods claimed the slights at the Navy facility were motivated by racism, the pint-sized player's superior skills as compared to the course cronies, and Lieutenant Colonel Woods's outranking most all of them. Tiger discussed the subject in Charles Barkley's book *Who's Afraid of a Large Black Man?*:

> For some reason all the white kids [at the Navy Golf Course] were
> allowed to play who were ten and under, though I wasn't. I had

people who were older—and I don't know if they were service-
men or retired or active or guests . . . I don't know who they
were—use the N word with me numerous times. I was there pitching, just pitching at a little chipping green. And they wanted to
pitch, so they would yell at me and I'd have to go to the putting
green. So I'd go to the putting green and I'd get yelled at over on
the putting green. I'd go back to the chipping green, then get
yelled at on the chipping green. These are things that obviously
hardened me a little bit and made me realize that golf was not
like basketball or football at the time. It was different, under different rules. Even traveling the country as a kid, I wasn't allowed
to go to certain pro shops or certain clubhouses to change shoes
where all the other kids were allowed to.

Tiger's purposeful distance from the world is understandable
when you consider how difficult it is to win the popular celebrity
game. Even Phil Mickelson is frequently criticized as being disingenuous because he is always so nice, enthusiastic, and accommo-
dating with the media and the fans. A flimsy 2006 *GQ* article, "The
Ten Most Hated Athletes," amazingly listed Mickelson as number eight, quoting an anonymous reporter's claim that "his peers
think he's preening and insincere." Memo: *of course* Phil's charming public persona is an act! Everything we do in public is an act.
In Phil's case, it's a darn good one, particularly in the context of
the general standard of behavior set by professional athletes. Phil's
carefully crafted "act" is appealing enough to the public and corporate sponsors to make him the third-highest paid athlete in the
world.

Howard Sounes took Tiger to task in *The Wicked Game* for
devoting "little of his time to the [Tiger Woods] Foundation—no
more than twenty days a year—and relatively little of his own
money." Of course the Tiger-hosted Target World Challenge and
AT&T National tournaments, Tiger Jam gala and headliner con-

cert in Las Vegas, and his numerous endorsement partnerships funnel millions into the foundation annually. The "relatively little of his own money" comment was pulled from IRS information about his direct contributions, obviously an insignificant sound bite extracted from a massively successful and complex charitable operation driven by Tiger's time, energy, celebrity, and wealth network. Tiger's "mere" twenty days of charity work for an active professional athlete with a virtually year-round competitive schedule likely ranks Tiger at or near the top among the select group of A+-level professional athletes (Andre Agassi and Lance Armstrong give similar amounts of time and energy to their charities). Sounes also took Tiger to task for moving to Florida at the beginning of his pro career (a hotbed for PGA Tour players because of the temperate climate and outstanding golf courses, convenience for both continental and international travel, and lack of state income tax). "If he was so concerned about common people [arguing the sincerity of his devotion to charitable causes], those people he grew up with in Cypress, he might have chosen to continue to reside in his home state and thereby give a portion of his enormous income back to the community, via the equitable and expeditious method of paying state income tax." Sounes concludes his riff with an unflattering comment on Tiger's reported penchant for high-stakes gambling: "He is said to play [blackjack] for $10,000 per hand—the amount his foundation donated to Denver Children's Hospital in 2000–2001, which puts his charitable work in perspective."

It also helps put the challenges of celebrity and generosity into perspective as a game that you just can't win. Tiger is compensated tremendously because he provides an irreplaceable economic benefit—in the form of sports entertainment—to society. Sure, he and the rest of our entertainers are grossly overpaid when you compare their wages and contributions to the advancement of society with those of schoolteachers. But we all have willfully agreed to play by the rules of capitalism in our free world, so it's hypocritical to criticize people for playing and winning the game.

Spending much of my workday exchanging e-mails, I'm amused at the different communication styles and how they reflect the sender's personality. After getting hit with the BlackBerry-style acronym-laced exchanges from busy, important types, I'm compelled to reflect on my own tendency toward thoughtful and detailed messages. Is this really the most productive way to communicate? Or could I consider a better strategy that saves time and energy and still keeps the plates spinning? We all have to reflect on what best promotes personal peak performance and maintain a sincere focus and commitment to acting accordingly and endure whatever difficult, emotionally charged consequences might arise.

For example, you might experience dysfunctional, disempowering conflict in your marriage. Psychologist and marriage researcher Dr. John Gottman says that marriage conflict itself is not the problem; instead, the problem is how we handle the conflict. Conflict and anger can actually be healing and balancing for a relationship. However, a relationship suffers in the presence of what Gottman calls the "Four Horsemen of the Apocalypse": criticism, contempt, defensiveness, and stonewalling. Because a relationship is an interaction between two people, it follows that if one person changes, the relationship can be transformed. If you get defensive or shut down in times of conflict, you could resolve to hear your partner out without challenge when a complaint is lodged. This would predict a more favorable response from your partner, healthier argument resolution, and a more successful relationship. Workplace distractions can be obliterated simply by establishing new communication guidelines with drop-in visitors or by exercising discipline when using e-mail, instant messaging, the telephone, and other tools or devices that can tend to interfere with your productivity and focus. A Silicon Valley software executive friend of mine answers his e-mail every *other* day; he is still able to thrive in the fastest paced business climate around. On the golf course, making a simple commitment such as warming up before every round or adopting a deliberate preshot routine (something every pro does with great discipline) could deliver a significant improvement in performance.

Pursuing Present Peak Performance in All Areas of Life

In one fell swoop we mention fixing your marriage, being more productive at work, and improving your golf game. Whew—sounds like a triathlete in training! Indeed, to lead a healthy, happy, balanced life and attain peak performance in varied goals, you have to nail your "transitions" like a triathlete. During a race, the triathlete's transitions from swimming to cycling and cycling to running involve much strategy and preparation to complete smoothly, as do the transitions between our various life roles. Unfortunately, the importance of transitions has been mostly disregarded in modern life, where it's more esteemed to multitask, be constantly wired and to travel, communicate, eat, and acquire stuff as quickly as possible.

There are many drawbacks associated with narrowly focused peak performers who ignore the big picture. The list of athletes who put up impressive numbers but alienate teammates and disrespect the rules of society is embarrassingly long. We have hundreds of professional athletes in the major sports (football, basketball, baseball, hockey) having their mug shots taken each year, NFL coaches praising intrasquad fights during training camp as a sign of competitive intensity, the egotistical behavior of Barry Bonds, Terrell Owens, Kobe Bryant, and their ilk, and of course the widespread doping in football, baseball, cycling, and track and field. Away from the public eye, we have droves of successful career folks who neglect their families or play loose with laws and morals in the name of winning and earning. If you are thumbing your BlackBerry at the breakfast table, absentmindedly nodding your head while your son is talking to you, you are practicing lousy focusing skills and missing out on those precious few minutes a day that represent the average period of parent-child quality time (experts and studies estimate in the range of ten to forty minutes per day of direct interaction without distractions of TV or other stimuli).

The great peak performance attributes of these flawed characters could easily be leveraged in other directions to bring victories. The athlete who rallies his team under pressure could do the same for his community instead of being a real-life nuisance. The executive who deftly balances the multifaceted demands of her time at work could do the same to meet the needs of her spouse, children, and personal health and fitness. To fully focus on each area of your life, you have to rise above the cultural forces that can deter you from smooth transitions and broad peak performance. Our easy access to communication technology might strengthen relationships challenged by time and distance, but it can just as easily lead to overload and distraction due to the incredible competition for our attention. Our endless pursuit of a higher standard of living corresponds to additional responsibilities, time, and hassles relating to caring for each incremental cool thing that we acquire.

Focusing and transitioning effectively requires tremendous discipline and devotion to the process; destructive shortcuts and distractions happen when we worry about results. Back to the metaphors, you must take your day shot by shot and enjoy each opportunity for peak performance. Be the ultimate, engaged father or mother at the breakfast table and on the walk to school. Then kiss your kid good-bye, flip the switch, and jabber on your iPhone till your tooth turns blue. Make time for a healthy lunch and snacks throughout the day instead of succumbing to the caffeine addiction, sugar fixes, and corresponding energy lulls that seem to be standard operating procedure in the workplace.

When it's time for some exercise, choose an activity and an effort level that feels comfortable and energizing, instead of trying to keep up with—and measure your self-worth by—the pace of the pack or the peppy teacher. Maximize workout benefits by getting outdoors and enjoying open space, fresh air, and a clear head. Appreciate heat, rain, wind, nature, getting lost, or meeting someone new on the trail as part of the adventure, instead of slaving away on yet another machine (treadmill, stationary bike, and the like) while the CNN broadcast from the hanging TVs helps disconnect mind from body.

If you are too busy for smooth and distinct transitions, you will suffer later. Once I was running side by side with an opponent on the third and final leg of a triathlon. After a mile of hard running, I couldn't hold my straight face any longer, so I turned and mentioned to him, "Hey, dude, your [bicycle] helmet is still on!" He reached up, cursed, and slowed down to fuss with the strap and remove the helmet while I sped ahead. If you compromise balance during your workday; skipping meals, exercise, and brief breaks from the screen to rejuvenate your eyes, muscles, and joints, you will assuredly get tired and lose focus at some point later in the day. It's true that time is inexorable, but it's also true that you can increase productivity by altering your work and lifestyle habits. The half hour you "lose" from exercising at lunchtime will pay back tenfold both in the workplace and also in a long, healthy, happy, balanced life.

Expect the Unexpected

The perils associated with a results obsession also extend to expectations about your competitive circumstances. When your mind-set and motivations are outward directed, your focus can be unsettled by numerous variables that don't go according to plan. At golf tournaments, the charming phenomenon of gallery roars can distract even the most focused player. As sounds emanate from other areas around the course, most players and other astute observers can determine who is being cheered (based on what hole the roar emanates from) and also what that player did (birdie = loud roar; trouble = loud groans; eagle = sustained deafening roar). Many a player has backed away from a putt when startled by a roar from a proximate hole. At that point, the champion has to discipline the mind to remain focused on the task at hand instead of wondering, worrying, or grieving about the event that caused the roar. Bad breaks are ubiquitous in golf, as well as in life. If you can accept that reality, you can overcome them much easier than if you dwell on them. Those who can truly internalize the admonition to expect the unexpected can gain a significant advantage over the wound-up competitor who needs everything to go according to plan in order to give himself a chance to thrive.

Remarkably, even the greatest athletes have trouble dealing with the unexpected. Granted, when one is focusing intently, it's no fun to get interrupted or disturbed. Sergio Garcia gave us a shockingly pathetic example of a poor attitude and mind-set at his press conference following his crushing defeat at the 2007 British Open at Royal Carnoustie. Garcia led from the outset and entered the final round with a three-shot lead after steady, disciplined play. Most observers thought his time had arrived to win his first major and finally fulfill the superstardom predicted of him since he was a teenager and placed runner-up to Tiger at the 1999 PGA.

Garcia's nerves intervened during the final round, and he struggled to a 2-over par-73 on a windless day where the course was there for the taking. Irishman Padraig Harrington gobbled up Garcia and amassed a one-shot lead by the eighteenth tee. In a frightening déjà vu of Jan Van de Velde's debacle on the same hole eight years earlier, Harrington proceeded to hit into the water twice on what many agree is the most difficult finishing hole in golf. Only a magnificent pitch and one-putt that salvaged double-bogey (and a 67) left him holding on to a little hope when Garcia reached the eighteenth with his own one-shot lead. Garcia needed par to win outright but could only muster bogey. The ensuing four-hole play-off was won by Harrington by one shot.

At the posttournament press conference, Harrington asserted with great intensity his champion mind-set, which helped him overcome the tremendous psycho-emotional wound of gagging the British Open spectacularly on the final hole. "I never, ever let myself feel like I lost the Open [after the final hole]. As I sat watching, I was as disciplined as I could be with my focus, not to brood or [think about] ifs and buts. I never let it cross my mind that I'd just blown the Open."

Garcia sounded a different tune afterward. Discussing his approach shot on the eighteenth, which he pulled into a bunker short and left of the green, he said, "I was hitting three-iron, so it was not an easy shot. Having to wait fifteen minutes to hit a shot when you are trying to win the British Open doesn't help. I wasn't very happy about that." Garcia was asked about his tee shot on the second play-off hole (the 248-yard, par-3 sixteenth), which hit the stick and caromed past the hole. "It's funny how some guys hit the pin and go in or go to a foot. Mine hits the pin and goes twenty feet away." Good point in Sergioland, but in reality, his three-iron was coming in hot and the stick clearly slowed it from going even farther past the hole. Sergio wasn't done: "You know what's the saddest thing about it? It's not the first time unfortunately. It's not the first time. Obviously, you [media] haven't been watching me that much. You only watch the guys that make the putts and get the good breaks and things like that."

Golf Channel TV analyst and former Tour player Brandel Chamblee made these pointed comments after the tournament: "They don't give major championships away. You have to earn them, with great skill and a sort of calmness in your head . . . evidenced by great shots. Players that don't live up to their potential let their past frustrations scar them. Sergio has had tremendous success in the game, but instead of thinking about that, he's thinking about his past failures; woe is me." The world's media chimed in with a loud chorus. MSNBC columnist Jim McCabe, in his scathing op-ed titled "Garcia needs more class, not talent," reminded us that "on many occasions [Arnold] Palmer would say that what molded his competitive life weren't the tournaments he won, but those he lost. He learned how to deal with the pain, learn from it, and become a better person."

"HE WAS SO FAR FROM BEING DISCONCERTED THAT HE TEASED A BIRDIE OUT OF THAT DIFFICULT PAR FIVE."

—Hugh McIllvanney

A fifteen-minute delay before hitting the final shot of the final round in golf's oldest and arguably greatest championship could have been perceived as an opportunity to appreciate one of the most intense athletic experiences that Sergio Garcia will ever have in his life. He could have added to his résumé the ability to keep his composure under the most trying circumstances instead of succumbing in more ways than one. Seven years prior at the same tournament, Tiger endured a thirty-six-minute delay on the fifth tee during the second round at St. Andrews. As Hugh McIllvanney observed in his *London Times* article, "Patience has been one of [Tiger's] most impressive characteristics. . . . He was so far from being disconcerted [about the wait] that he teased a birdie out of that difficult par five [after play resumed]. . . . While waiting[,] . . . Woods had been the essence of relaxation. He ate a snack bar and chatted with his playing partners. . . . He was sufficiently free of tension to converse about subjects far removed from the urgent concerns of the moment."

Tiger certainly would have been less chatty had he been waiting on the seventy-second hole like Sergio, but the lesson still holds: you absolutely cannot allow yourself to lose focus based on competitive surprises, bad breaks, or anything else unexpected. If Paddy Harrington can steel his mind immediately after a devastating ordeal in front of millions on the seventy-second hole while leading the British Open, you can do it after a bad hole at your member-guest invitational, or after a harsh exchange with your boss about the quality of your work, or when you get a C on your report instead of the A you expected. What comes as second nature to Tiger might be an extremely laborious effort for you and me, but you can do it—and you have done it on the many occasions in your life where you triumphed over adversity.

Funnyman Martin Lawrence delivered a hilarious and also vulnerable stand-up performance/feature film called *Runteldat* on the heels of a few highly publicized health and legal troubles. His tagline "no one is immune to the trials and tribulations of life" is worth reflecting upon regularly. We are being constantly programmed to believe that we can avoid trials and tribulations by buying something—prescription drugs, comfort food, a new blouse, a miracle antiaging cream, teeth whitener, a set of irons, a Hummer, or a home in a gate-guarded community. Skate through your years without adversity and grow old surrounded by your possessions—what a deal! This, of course, is the great lie of Madison Avenue. You may not be inclined to push your body to collapse to discover the meaning of struggle like Bannister, but we must all realize that "the urge to struggle lies latent in everyone" and appreciate the value of pursuing peak performance through adversity.

Get Out of Your Own Way

A friend recently characterized his golf round on vacation as follows: "I had a triple-bogey on the second hole and never recovered." In the real world, we humans revel in the trafficking of complaints, excuses, commiserating, blame, and self-limiting beliefs. If you meet someone at a party and forget his or her name, you might venture forward saying, "I'm sorry. I'm terrible with names. What's yours again?" This positions your subconscious to remain mired in poor name recognition. You could choose a more empowering stance and open with, "I'm working really hard on remembering names, and I'm sorry I forgot yours. Please tell me again."

When you need help with your spreadsheet, do you say to a coworker, "Oh, I hate this stupid Excel! Can you help me?" and then sit back and sigh while she fixes things for you? Or do you sit forward with pen and notepad in hand, eager to learn some new tricks that will help you navigate smoother waters in the future? With the former kind of attitude, you might navigate your way through your day adequately, but you do not even sniff at peak performance. Mark Allen, the greatest triathlete in history and six-time winner of the Hawaii Ironman, said in his book *Total Triathlete*, "Unless you test yourself, you stagnate. Unless you try to go way beyond what you've been able to do before, you won't develop and grow. When you go for it 100%, when you don't have the fear of 'what if I fail,' that's when you learn. That's when you're really living."

In college, I was struggling one day with math homework (from a "Math for Nonmajors" class, go figure) and by chance was being visited by my friend Steve Kobrine, a certified math whiz who earned a B.S. from UC Berkeley at age nineteen. He graciously offered to lend a hand with my work that looked suspiciously like high school algebra. "I'm sorry, I haven't seen these kinds of problems since junior high," he said, trying mightily to not be condescending. What ensued was not so much a lesson in math as one in attitude. Out loud, he facilitated a critical-thinking process that led us together to the solutions. His higher math skills were entirely inapplicable to these problems—it might as well have been Spanish (except that Steve is terrible with Spanish)—but his confidence and eagerness to solve math problems were the requisite skills to deliver peak performance.

It seems our daily encounters with competitive circumstances are so loaded with self-imposed and society-imposed pressures and judgments that we sabotage our chances at peak performance before we even start. The jabbering on the first tees everywhere about shoulder injuries; lack of practice time; fears such as hitting the ball into water hazards or out of bounds, losing bets, letting our partner down, holding up the group behind us; or dealing with one-hundred-degree heat are so commonplace that it's truly frightening for humanity. Not as frightening as global warming but nevertheless destructive to the human spirit. With all the talk about the oppressive heat at the 2007 PGA Championship in Tulsa, Oklahoma, Tiger adopted a winning strategy, as he described in his August 2007 e-mail newsletter. "I down-played the heat at Southern Hills [it was over 100 degrees with high humidity, generating a heat index—"feels like"—value of 110] because if you dwell on it, it can drain you mentally and physically. It was brutally hot, but the humidity wasn't as bad as Florida. I just refused to let it get to me and felt as fresh walking up to the 18th green Sunday as I did walking off the first tee Thursday. Stevie [Williams] did a great job on the bag, and kept me hydrated and as dry as possible."

What if—for a golf round, an entire day, or a week or even longer—we were able to discard all of our excuses and lay down our coats of armor protecting us from ego slights, embarrassment, and the reopening of emotional wounds that occurred in childhood when someone told us we weren't good enough? We could then compete for fun, to free the human spirit and to bring meaning and richness to our lives through the struggle. Focus would come effortlessly.

The Secret Is in the Dirt

Regarding the particulars of how to get to peak performance in your own life, there are no big secrets. You can buy a ton of books on the subjects of your interest, from the heavy scientific-analytic texts to Hollywood rah-rah fodder, with Suzanne Somers leading the pack spouting oxymoronic blurbs like, "Eat incredible, rich foods in abundant portions while the unwanted pounds effortlessly melt away." The endless distractions of the digital age (Tony Robbins says, "It's not a digital age, it's an entertainment age") can lead us astray from the simplicity of pursuing peak performance until one day you discover that you're spending all of your time strategizing, analyzing, purchasing, and consuming instead of creating anything. Google cofounder Sergey Brin related in a *Business 2.0* magazine interview that even in the world of technology, "Simplicity is an important trend we are focused on. Technology has a way of becoming overly complex, but simplicity was one of the reasons people gravitated to Google initially . . . success will come from simplicity."

For most of us, it's a matter of discarding various unproductive elements of our approach rather than acquiring new information. Turn off the BlackBerry to become a better mom or dad. Eliminate self-limiting beliefs and reframe them into positive and empowering stances. Resist the momentum directing you toward inactivity, consumerism, lottery dreams, and unchallenged aging of mind and body. Discard overly regimented diets and overly stressful exercise programs in favor of eating healthy, natural foods and engaging in fun, energizing physical activity of your preference.

IT'S A MATTER OF DISCARDING VARIOUS UNPRODUCTIVE ELEMENTS OF OUR APPROACH RATHER THAN ACQUIRING NEW INFORMATION.

Instead of searching outside yourself for a "secret" for sale in some store, adopt a simple approach to peak performance. Remember that all the great exploits of Tiger emanate from years and years of devoted, highly repetitive practice and repeated exposure to intense competition. At his press conference before the 2006 Target World Challenge, Tiger offered this advice to amateur golfers wishing to improve: "When it comes to amateurs, practice. You know, my father always used to tell me, you get out of it what you put into it. If you work hard, you're going to get results. But if you don't put any effort, you didn't put any work into it, you don't bust your butt, you won't get any results; and more importantly, you don't deserve any." As the classic quote from the late golf legend Ben Hogan goes (when he was asked the secret to his golf success), "The secret is in the dirt [of the practice range]."

TIPS FOR IMPROVING YOUR FOCUS

1. Create an ideal peak performance environment. Take the mechanical steps necessary to promote success. Choose endeavors that are aligned with your highest goals, so that you are ready to be your best every time you compete. String up the gallery ropes to help maintain focus. Respect the importance of a routine, like Tiger before each round and each shot, and of being prepared. Carry your figurative umbrella and rain gear just in case.

2. Have the courage and discipline to make difficult decisions. You must do so in the interest of your peak performance, health, and happiness. This includes communicating honestly and directly in difficult relationships or severing them if necessary. Develop an optimum peak performance style that is true to your basic nature and aligned with your goals.

3. Pursue peak performance in all areas of life. Focusing only on career or athletic performance brings numerous drawbacks, while applying your skills to other challenges and responsibilities creates leverage that supports broad success and happiness. Focus on making smooth transitions from one life responsibility to another; blurring the lines compromises performance in each and creates additional stress.

4. Expect the unexpected. When you appreciate the rewards of pursuing peak performance regardless of outcome, you will not be tripped up when competitive circumstances don't go according to plan. Trials, tribulations, and even defeat represent powerful growth opportunities.

5. Get out of your own way. Much of our difficulty in focusing stems from our own negative attitudes and actions. Cultivate a positive attitude toward your goals and discard destructive beliefs and behavior patterns to attain the ideal competitive mind-set. Maintain a simple approach and an understanding that hard work produces results.

David Cannon/Getty Images

4

TIGER SUCCESS FACTOR 2
WORK-PLAY ETHIC

The character trait of a strong work ethic has long been attached to winners, but I believe it's incomplete and outdated today. The work-play ethic embodied by Tiger means he loves his work so much that it feels like play. This represents a more powerful level of functioning than seen in someone who puts his head down and doggedly clocks his hours, forgetting the importance of fun. One can certainly be successful when driven by superficials such as money and ego or even by negative feelings such as low self-worth, anger at feeling slighted, or other internal demons. However, these sources of motivation are less resilient than intrinsic motivators—things that get exposed when competitive circumstances become more challenging.

Tiger's work-play ethic means he loves to compete, he loves to win and hates to lose, but he is able to gain the biggest rush from the battle and release his attachment to the outcome. In an engaging 2006 interview with the late Ed Bradley on "60 Minutes," Tiger explained, "I love to compete—whatever it is. You and I could be playing cards right now, and I'd want to kick your butt." "You'd wanna win?" Bradley prodded. "No, I'd wanna kick your butt, there's a difference. It's just in me, I don't know why. I enjoy competing."

In a joint interview with Tiger and Mark O'Meara that appeared in the January 1999 *Golf Digest*, O'Meara related a story of a friendly golf match where Tiger won $30 and was adamant about getting paid immediately, while still on the final green, simply to revel in the moment and rub in his victory. To Tiger, the thirty bucks on its own is not worth bending over to pick up and put in his wallet (because, you see, it takes longer than ten seconds to do this—with 31.5 million seconds in a year, Tiger's $112 million annual income equates to earnings of $3.55 per second). Whether its thirty bucks or thirty million, the money is secondary to the symbolism behind the superficial prizes that Tiger acquires along his journey, which, by the way, has no finish line. As he told Ed Bradley, "I love to practice. In the summertime, it's 'have light, will play'— sometimes as much as fourteen hours. There's always stuff to work on. You never, ever arrive. But it sure is fun trying. . . . To me, work is fun."

In Charles P. Pierce's *GQ* article, Butch Harmon riffed on Tiger's three greatest golf attributes: his athletic build and swing, the expert early teachings of Earl, and his ability to have fun with golf. "You know, you can get so wrapped up in this game that you have no fun, and as soon as you know it, your career is over and you never had any. It's a game you can get so serious on that you can't . . . play," said Harmon, by way of explaining that Tiger indeed knows how to "play" the game. We're all familiar with the hugs and fist bumps that Tiger shares with longtime caddie and good friend Steve Williams after great shots and great victories. Once, however, the duo curiously exchanged a high five *before* Tiger hit a shot—on the seventeenth hole of the second round at the 2000 British Open. Dan Jenkins asked Tiger about this in a September 2000 story in *Golf Digest*. "Were [you] celebrating the discovery of a decent lie? 'No, we were just telling jokes,' Tiger related."

Cultivating the Work-Play Ethic

Tiger's advantage is stepping into the competitive arena with the innocence and exuberance of a child, unburdened by the expectations placed on him by the public and the media. His emotional distance from the media and even fans on the golf course could be a product of what David Owen described in *The Chosen One* as follows: "We feel exalted when we watch great athletes perform, but our reaction is at least partly paradoxical, because great athletes are the ultimate narcissists. Their focus is inward, and it is purely selfish."

TIGER'S ADVANTAGE IS STEPPING INTO THE COMPETITIVE ARENA WITH THE INNOCENCE AND EXUBERANCE OF A CHILD, UNBURDENED BY THE EXPECTATIONS PLACED ON HIM BY THE PUBLIC AND THE MEDIA.

However, you could easily spin this logic to argue that Tiger's focus is *selfless*; he is so committed to greatness that his own ego gratification is secondary to his mission to raise the bar—not only for his own curiosity and edification but for all golfers, athletes, and kids inside the Tiger Woods Learning Center walls and outside the walls across the entire planet. When Tiger said, "The only thing I can do is try to give back. If it works, it works," he was talking about his foundation efforts. But as we reflect on his superhuman achievements and transcendent goals, the statement could capture his entire life purpose, as Earl argued vehemently to anyone who would listen—and impressed passionately upon Tiger his entire life. This might seem like fluffy or circular logic, but how else to explain the performances of an athlete who has proven time and again not only to be immune to pressure but to thrive on it so improbably? Ponder that and the truth that Tiger's competitive fire has not been compromised in the slightest by the accumulation of massive wealth, titles, and accolades, and it's clear his commitment extends far beyond the typical athlete trying to make a name and nest egg for himself.

Ed Bradley expanded on the "work is fun" point with Tiger. "On the golf course, in a tournament, you're looking to kick some butt. But you do it with such a nice smile!" Tiger answered, "Well, technically, if you're kicking butt, you should be smiling. I enjoy that rush of trying to beat these guys. These guys are the best in the world and I'm very lucky to have that opportunity to try and compete against the best in the world. That's why you see me smiling out there. It's a rush!"

At a press conference before the 2007 British Open, Tiger explained why it's his favorite major championship. "I love playing over here, because it allows you to be creative." Regarding his first exposure to British-style "links" golf (meaning land linked to the ocean, featuring landscapes that are typically extremely windy and treeless—thus offering completely different challenges than found on the lush, American-style golf course), where he struggled to a 9-over par, forty-eighth-place finish in the Scottish Open as a nineteen-year-old amateur, Tiger remembered, "I absolutely loved it. It was the first time I could actually use the ground. I grew up on kikuyu grass golf courses (in California), and you never would bump-and-run a golf ball there. I thought it was neat to putt from 40 to 50 yards off the green, hit a five-iron from 135 yards and run the ball. That to me was fun." Newsflash for the unenlightened: "Tiger has fun in forty-eighth place, and you can, too!"

Did I catch you here defaulting to thinking, "Easy for him to say, he's a budding billionaire. If I don't close these two big deals this quarter, I'm gonna miss my quota." I'll concede that Tiger makes things that ain't so simple look simple on the grand stage. It's terribly difficult to get out of your own way, shake the shadow of your ego's demands and emotional scars, and just grip it and rip it, as John Daly (colorful Tour player famous for his long drives, go-for-broke strategy, excessive lifestyle, enduring battle with alcohol and gambling addictions, domestic strife with multiple wives, and so on) would say. But there is great value in the simplicity of Tiger's example, the kid with the big smile and the giant fist pump who has loved the compelling challenge offered by the game of golf since he was eleven months old.

There are plenty of other examples. Michael Jordan had to have the ball at the end of the game, infatuated with the love of the battle and the opportunity to decide the game, win or lose. The Google founders, Sergey Brin and Larry Page, eschewed the quick money of the dot-com public-offering craze in order to remain focused and in control of their dream of building the world's greatest search engine without compromise or distraction. A baby learning to walk pulls herself up again and again, persevering after repeated failures in a completely natural expression of the indomitable human spirit.

Friendly Rivalries

There are numerous stories of Tiger's playful approach to golf behind the scenes. David Owen's *Men's Vogue* piece details how Tiger went to elaborate lengths to stage a practical joke on Tour comrade Mike Weir. They were at a video game footage capture session on a Hollywood soundstage; Tiger was in the wardrobe area getting dressed. Owen relates, "As Woods put on the sleeveless T-shirt, he noticed another on the rack, an extremely small one, perhaps meant for a petite woman, and had an idea: It would be funny, he decided, to trick Weir into wearing the tiny shirt, get a photographer to surreptitiously take a picture of him in it, give a print to a child in the gallery at some future tournament, and have the child (with Woods watching) ask Weir to autograph it. Woods looked over his shoulder to make sure that Weir wasn't nearby and said to the technicians, 'You guys have to help me out on this. Tell him that [his shirt] has to be as tight as possible—almost so it hurts.' "

Mark O'Meara, one of Tiger's closest friends on Tour and a father-figure type given their nineteen-year age difference, has related at length the positive impact Tiger and his youthful, competitive spirit had on his career. Prior to hanging with Tiger, O'Meara's sixteen years on Tour were marked by consistent performances, fourteen victories, and tons of prize money, but he was nevertheless considered an underachiever by many. Then a mutually beneficial relationship blossomed when Tiger left college and moved, all alone, to Isleworth, Florida, to launch his pro career in late 1996. Tom Callahan relates Tiger's reflections in *In Search of Tiger*: "He [O'Meara] kind of took me aside and showed me the ropes of life away from college. . . . You come home to your house and no one's there. How do you get over the loneliness factor of playing and practicing so much golf? Marko basically opened up his arms and his house to me and said, 'Come be a part of our family.' "

In 1998 O'Meara earned a breakout victory at the Masters (his first major), birdieing three of the final four holes to surprise David Duval and Fred Couples. He followed that up with another major victory at the British Open, where he and Brian Watts finished one shot ahead of Tiger and went to a four-hole play-off, which O'Meara won by two shots. He closed the season with another outstanding performance at the PGA Championship, tying for fourth place.

The distinctive element of the Woods-O'Meara relationship is the productive blending of their intense competitive natures with fun and friendship. As each other's foil, they spurred a mutual escalation of passion for the game. O'Meara commented in a January 1999 *Golf Digest* joint interview with Tiger,

> If he hadn't moved in, I'm not so sure I would have won the Masters and the British Open [in 1998]. I might never have won a major championship professionally. The youth and the enthusiasm he carries, and his competitiveness, maybe just made it burn a little bit more inside me, thinking, "Hey, even though Tiger is twenty-two and he can do things with a golf ball that I can't do, maybe if I get into a position where I have a chance and finally put everything together" . . . For years everyone was saying "Why doesn't Mark O'Meara win a major?" . . . I enjoy a challenge as much as he enjoys a challenge. Like when I'm out there on a par 4 and I hit a good drive. I might be 185 yards out, and I'll hit a four-iron. I know he's up there hitting a seven-iron. I know he's got the big advantage. So I'll hit one in there like this [extends hands indicating a shot close to the hole], and I'll yell up to him, "Tiger, did you see that one? Is it on the green? I'm forty-one; I don't see as well anymore. Where did that ball go?" I know he's thinking, "This old guy has done it to me again."

In the conversation, they relate another interesting passage about their friendly rivalry when they faced each other at the 1998 World Match Play Championship finals. Tiger had already amassed a big lead by the eleventh hole when O'Meara hit a great approach shot to eighteen inches, while Tiger hit his to thirty-five feet. After Tiger missed his putt, O'Meara conceded the next putt. Common courtesy in match play dictates that Tiger would in turn concede O'Meara's putt, allowing O'Meara to win the hole. O'Meara remembers the interaction. "[Tiger] hadn't said a whole lot to that point. He wasn't going to talk unless I said anything. He had his game face on pretty good. . . . I'm thinking, 'This is strange. He's going to make me putt this.' When I put my ball down, he's still walking off the green. I called over. He says, 'What?' I said, 'Are you kidding me? You give me these at home. Are you crazy?' That kinda loosened up the whole thing. He looked at me, smiled, and said, 'Hey, putt it.' I knew then exactly how I stood." Tiger added, "He hadn't won a hole yet. Really, what I wanted to happen, did. He started to worry a little about me instead of the putt. I started to get into his head. There was a little gamesmanship going on. I really wanted to win, and I know he did, too."

Swing Changes

Mark Kreidler, author and sports columnist for ESPN.com, captured Tiger's work-play ethic when he wrote, "Tiger Woods is the greatest force in the modern history of the sport, so confident that he is willing to remake his game even while in the midst of his greatest successes, so strict in adherence to his goals that he long ago moved past the shadowy area of popularity and on into pure purpose. . . . What they see is a player who remade his swing not once but twice, and both times despite already achieving some staggering success. They see an athlete who trains at the highest levels of fitness despite playing a sport that can produce a legitimate competitor like, say, John Daly. They certainly see a person who came to grips early on with his talent and has never appeared remotely afraid to take responsibility for his career."

Tiger's lauded, but at the time heavily criticized, swing overhauls were rooted in a desire to improve, regardless of his standing on the world rankings or the short-term consequence of diminished performance. His first overhaul came on the heels of the 1997 Masters victory, possibly the second-greatest golfing performance in history behind his 2000 U.S. Open. About his intensive review of tournament video, Tiger said, "I didn't see one flaw . . . I saw ten! I knew I wasn't in the greatest positions in my swing. But my timing was great, so I got away with it. And I made almost every putt. You can have a wonderful week like that even when your swing isn't sound.

But can you still contend in tournaments with that swing when your timing isn't good? Will it hold up over a long period of time? The answer to those questions, with the swing I had, was no. And I wanted to change that." In the process, he was able to step outside of his own ego, the planet's hysteria over his Masters performance, and the socialization of the modern athlete to be all-powerful, all-knowing, egocentric, and quite often deluded.

This swing reconstruction lasted from late 1997 until early 1999. In 1998 Tiger won only one PGA Tour event and endured heavy criticism about his decision to retool. He knew what he was doing, however, for 1999 marked the beginning of the greatest streak of golf ever played: nineteen wins in forty-three tournaments, four consecutive major victories, six consecutive PGA Tour wins, and all-time records for U.S. and British Open scores, season scoring average, annual prize money, and, perhaps most remarkable, going an unfathomable sixty-three holes without a single bogey during the two most severe tests of golf in the world: the U.S. and British Opens. The streak started on the tenth hole of round three in the U.S. Open and extended through the second hole of round three at the British Open at St. Andrews a few weeks later.

Tiger's second swing overhaul, supposedly prompted by the desire to reduce stress on his surgically repaired knee, came in 2003 with new teacher Hank Haney. What followed was another Tiger slump: he lost the world's number-one ranking (held for a record 264 consecutive weeks) to Vijay Singh in September 2004, failed to win a major in 2003 and 2004, and once again (will they ever learn?) endured heavy criticism from the pundits for fooling with perfection. Alas, the new swing started clicking for the 2005 season, and Tiger enjoyed another incredible tear—returning to the number-one ranking; winning the 2005 Masters and U.S. Opens, the 2006 British Open and PGA, and his last six tournaments of 2006; placing second, second, twelfth, and first in the major championships of 2007; winning the new 2007 FedEx Cup play-offs and

Tour Championship by a mile; and winning twenty-two times out of fifty tournaments through 2007.

Learning How to Play All Over Again

We face heavy adversity in the pursuit of this work-play ethic in the form of the harsh and judgmental modern world. Babies grow up to play little league, try out for talent shows, take standardized exams, and ask the object of their attraction out on a date. At some point along the road, someone tells us or we discover for ourselves that we're not good enough. Years later, we rub our eyes and discover that we are out there banging the keyboard, pounding nails, making cold calls, raising kids, paying bills, watching others pursue their dreams on "American Idol," buying lottery tickets, and just getting through the day. Play—what's that?

The more serious and competitive a golfer gets, the more likelihood there is that a golf round—a journey of diverse physical challenges (strength and power, timing and rhythm, balance and intensive hand-eye coordination), mental challenges (problem solving, emotional control, sustained concentration), communing with nature, and enjoying the company of others—is reduced to a single number: "I shot a 76." From the very beginning, our self-esteem is dependent upon what we accomplish, not on the subtleties of what kind of character, sportsmanship, and empathy we display in competitive environments or what kind of karma and happiness we generate and radiate to the world. It's no wonder that fear and self-sabotage kick in when self-esteem and personal honor are on the line in a competitive setting.

Self-sabotagers are the ones who show up late or without proper equipment, thereby relieving pressure and expectations off the bat. Others repeat the same mistakes over and over, preferring to remain comfortably mediocre instead of taking risks and exploring ways to improve, as in, "I hate how poorly I putt, but I also hate practicing putting" or "I hate the morning rush hour, but I also hate getting up early to beat traffic." In these cases, our complaining, excuses, and self-limiting beliefs serve the important purpose of validating our guilty conscience. You're a lousy putter, but you're also upset about it, so you're still a tough competitor. You blew your diet and pigged out on dessert, but you feel guilty about it—hence, you're not an undisciplined slob but a devoted dieter who made a mistake and will inflict the appropriate self-punishment tomorrow. In contrast, a champion such as Tiger faces mistakes and shortcomings without negative self-judgment. Instead, he implements a proactive plan of attack and sees the "issues" at hand not as negatives but as opportunities for self-improvement.

Watching Tiger's competitive rounds, you may note that he is not standing on the bluffs marveling at the breaking waves or gazing at the beautiful flowers nor engaging the crowd with humorous antics like comedian Bill Murray does annually at Pebble Beach. But Tiger is appreciating the battle with boundless enthusiasm and passion, with a disposition that is closer to "play" than that of nearly anyone else out there. You can bet that Tiger relished being seven shots back with seven holes remaining at Pebble Beach in 2000 a heck of a lot more than marginal player Matt Gogel did being the leader, when Gogel experienced the agony of Tiger improbably catching and passing him for the victory. Why should it be that way? Gogel could have relished the opportunity to try and hold off the game's greatest player, win or lose. Succeeding would make his first Tour victory a hundred times sweeter than a less dramatic final nine holes, while a loss would provide a valuable growth experience. Unfortunately, a switch too often flips, despite our protests, when we're under pressure, and we freeze up like a deer in the headlights. Sufficiently deflated by Tiger passing him, Gogel gagged a short putt on the final hole that cost him more than a hundred grand for dropping from solo second place to a tie for second with Vijay Singh.

Why didn't Gogel's anticlimactic putt on eighteen merit the same focus as the putt he sank to assume the lead on Saturday or to extend his lead from six to seven shots on the front nine on Sunday? If we can examine where we are coming from and why, and perhaps make tiny adjustments to our mentality and perspective, we can slowly unlock more passion and competitive resilience. Fortunately, Gogel was able to assimilate the Tiger thrashing in a positive manner, coming back to Pebble Beach two years later and winning with some clutch play down the stretch.

The work-play ethic originates with a pure motivation. The real-estate agent who is driven by dollar signs is going to experience ebbs and flows of motivation and work ethic based on external circumstances such as market conditions and win-loss record. Pursuing success for success's sake can breed loosening morals, impatience, an imbalanced lifestyle, and even complacency when you cash enough checks. Failure can breed negativity and apathy so that the daily grind becomes just that. An agent motivated by the high ideal of helping people realize the American dream will have a powerful and unwavering motivation and work ethic. Success comes in the forming of strong emotional connections and deep appreciation over what is the most important financial transaction in most people's lives. The commissions that the agent gets when escrows close are merely pieces of the big puzzle, by-products of a pure motivation to deliver dreams. Hey, some years you make twenty-four dreams come true and qualify for the president's club trip to Hawaii, and other years it's only nine dreams, but that doesn't have to compromise your passion or focus. Similarly for Tiger, golf is, in his own words, merely a vehicle to "help and change [people] in a positive way."

Pushing Your Limits for Peak Performance

Unfortunately, many of us have trouble accepting the responsibility mentioned by Mark Kreidler—to pursue the highest expression of your talents and give yourself a fair shot at reaching and functioning at your potential. We stick with the same old swing—that is, the same destructive behavior patterns, relationship dynamics, excuses, and run-of-the-mill job—making a moderate effort and producing moderate results for a moderate salary. Technological progress and our increasing standard of living placates us such that the leather recliner and plasma-screen TV ("Buy now—No payments, no interest till 2009!") offer pleasant inertia against pushing our limits. Our focus drifts gently but sadly over time from peak performance to just making it through the day and enjoying the decadent spoils awarded for completing this modest challenge.

ALMOST ALL OF US WOULD GAIN GREAT MEANING AND RICHNESS IN OUR LIVES IF WE TOOK SOME BIG RISKS AND PURSUED EXTREME CHALLENGES.

There is nothing wrong with balancing an ambitious life with rest and relaxation—in fact, it's essential for peak performance. However, almost all of us would gain great meaning and richness in our lives if we took some big risks and pursued extreme challenges. As Mark Twain advocated, "Everything in moderation, including moderation." Think of the stakes Tiger anted up when he dismantled the golf swing that made him the richest and most famous athlete in the world. And yet you and I and our next-door neighbors will hesitate to quit our miserable jobs and start our own businesses, trapped by fear of uncertainty and failure or perhaps bought off by corporate America. We are training the younger generation to think this way, too, so that a disturbingly greater percentage of today's college kids choose their major based on future economic prospects instead of passion for learning, and young athletes will look pensively to the sideline after a bad play to see if they're getting yanked or further domesticated by criticism on the go.

You owe it to yourself and the world to discard moderation in this context and pursue peak performance with passion and courage, regardless of your fears about painful results. In his popular self-help book *The Celestine Prophecy*, James Redfield details a series of insights that, when observed and implemented into daily life, can produce a collective evolution of human consciousness. One insight mentions how we unconsciously compete for energy from others, a dynamic that underlies all conflict. "As we begin to become aware of these power struggles, we learn that there is, in reality, no lack of energy—there is another greater source of endless energy," argues Redfield. While Tiger's peers are mired in this energy struggle, battling opponents for prize checks and trophies, he has transcended it by striving for constant improvement—for unattainable perfection—on the golf course. This compelling goal represents a source of endless energy for him. He pursues this goal with a clean consciousness and pure motivation, devoid of issues such as insecurity, fear, monetary greed, and fluctuating self-esteem that plague even the world's greatest competitors.

Redfield's later insights detail how we are negatively impacted by carrying baggage from childhood emotional traumas and how we can transcend them by paying closer attention to our intuition and making productive connections with others—eliminating negative relationships in the process. The predicted outcome is this evolution in consciousness, with an implied by-product of widespread peak performance.

Working on transcending energy struggles and emotional hang-ups might not be as titillating as buying the new Nike SUMO Squared driver for four bills in the pro shop or thumbing through the photos in Tiger's *How I Play Golf* instruction book, but it is in this area where you can make the biggest dents in your handicap (pun intended).

WHILE TIGER'S PEERS ARE MIRED IN THIS ENERGY STRUGGLE, BATTLING OPPONENTS FOR PRIZE CHECKS AND TROPHIES, HE HAS TRANSCENDED IT BY STRIVING FOR CONSTANT IMPROVEMENT—FOR UNATTAINABLE PERFECTION—ON THE GOLF COURSE.

Take a glance at your own life and ponder how the various energy struggles you partake in are serving you. What's in that backpack you've been carrying around since elementary school and how does it impact your everyday life? Are there some things that have served their purpose but can now be discarded in the interest of evolving? For example, we construct elaborate defense mechanisms to protect our egos from the pain of criticism and failure. But maybe your mechanism—which served a purpose and provided some form of payoff to help you get through life—is inhibiting your continued growth.

Redfield calls these mechanisms "control dramas" and maintains that we each fall into one of the four categories according to our psycho-emotional needs or when presented with stressful or con-tentious situations: the poor me (getting attention and therefore power, or coping with stress, by eliciting sympathy and guilt through complaining and telling sob stories), the aloof (manipulating others and sucking energy by being distant, noncommittal, and withholding), the interrogator (seeking power and control with incessant questioning and criticism), and the intimidator (seeking power and compliance through fear, intimidation, and bullying).

When you pay closer attention to your behavior and identify your control dramas and those of others close to you, you can transcend the silly game of energy struggles and handle difficult situations by sharing energy and love instead of fighting for it. Surely you can reference real-life examples of both in negative interactions and success stories where you stepped out of your control drama and achieved breakthroughs in performance or emotional disposition—for example, the poor me who stops feeling sorry for himself and takes decisive action to improve his life; the aloof expressing her feelings, rather than withdrawing, during emotionally charged conversations; the interrogator relaxing, trusting, delegating, and teaching others; or the intimidator stepping up to become an effective leader by listening, empathizing, and empowering.

Discard Harmful Programming and Cultivate a Pure Motivation

The puritanical work ethic that defined the postwar generation, followed by the explosion of affluence and consumerism in recent generations, has contributed to disrespect of the "play" component of the work-play ethic in all walks of society. The weight-loss issue reveals the masses forcing their bodies through exercise regimens that are overly stressful and not enjoyable, coupled with diets based on deprivation and restriction. Their heroine Suzanne Somers espouses the attitude, "When it comes to fitness, I like to do as little as possible to stay in great shape. . . . I'm a lazy athlete!" Then the lazy athlete disciples wonder why they are not able to maintain their weight, a sensible healthy diet, nor a regular, energizing exercise program. The "work" ethic may be there, temporarily, but both motivation and goals are flawed.

Endurance sports are littered with high-achieving, goal-oriented, type-A enthusiasts who tend to be more committed to obsessive-compulsive overtraining than they are to peak performance. Numerous articles mention the perils caused by today's overbearing parenting style relating to extremely competitive college admissions. The consequent demand for students to excel in the narrow parameters of test performance and grade point average coupled with excessive parental involvement have created a generation of youth who lack creativity and self-responsibility. A 2006 *Newsweek* article called "The Fine Art of Letting Go," which discussed the phenomenon of "helicopter parents," quotes a Midwestern dean, who said, "There are cases where the parent tells the [college admissions] adviser that [his] son wants to be a doctor, and these are the classes he wants to take, and then, when the parent leaves the room, the student says 'I'm not sure I want to be a doctor at all. English and art are more interesting to me.'"

The familiar horror stories of overly competitive youth sports offer more examples where an adult-mandated work ethic overrides the importance of play, self-discovery, and choosing one's own path. Fast-rising PGA Tour player Sean O'Hair has remarkably triumphed over a dysfunctional and abusive relationship with his father, Marc. From a young age, Marc pushed Sean with a military-style training program and tightly controlled, golf-obsessed lifestyle (Marc sold his business in Lubbock, Texas, and moved the family to Florida to enroll Sean in the famed Leadbetter Golf Academy for precocious and driven talents). Sean endured much verbal abuse and a notorious regimen of having to run a postround mile for every bogey shot in tournament rounds. After one such seven-mile run on a treadmill, a fellow player remembers, "He could barely walk the next day." Sean severed his relationship with his father in 2002. Now

Marc is suing Sean for ten percent of his big income as an established Tour player—remuneration for Marc's ambitious estimate of $2 million in "training expenses" forked out during the developmental years. There are millions of other less dramatic cases where kids are blindly pursuing the goal of pleasing others or are perhaps so disconnected from their own dreams and desires they don't even realize they're missing out.

Developing a work-play ethic will likely require unwinding extensive harmful programming that you have been fed all your life. A friend of mine, an extremely high achiever (a graduate of an elite university who has a distinguished career as a business executive and also became an accomplished amateur endurance athlete, balancing family through it all), confirmed how difficult this can be. He said, "I don't know how to play. I can't do it. I just stand and watch while my family plays. I can't join. I try, but I just end up standing there not doing anything. I don't get it. As a kid, playing wasn't a choice. My life was structured into 'right things' and 'stupid worthless things' and I didn't know how to rebel, so I bought the story. Now my mind yells at me to do 'right things' only, no worthless things allowed. Even though I get this insanity intellectually, the yelling voice is louder than my intellectual self. How do I know what I like? I only know what's acceptable."

Peeling away harmful programming can happen wonderfully one layer at a time. Take a little risk today and do something just for the fun of it—even something trivial such as wrestling a bone out of your dog's mouth—rather than because it's expected or demanded of you. (David Owen mentioned Tiger's affection for his border collie Taz in his 2006 *Men's Vogue* piece. "[Tiger] has a picture of Taz on his cell phone, refers to himself as 'Daddy,' and took time out to roll around on the floor of his office when he was already running late.")

"It's much harder than you think," continues my friend about rejecting the lifelong results-oriented programming. "You have to convince yourself that the guilt is bullshit, realizing that what you've internalized came from outside when you were young and it isn't real, it just feels real." What might provide some incentive is to look at the seemingly paradoxical success enjoyed by those who "play" for a living. When Tiger shot his record-tying 63 in the second round of the 2007 PGA, he missed a heartbreaking putt on the final hole that would have set a new low-round scoring record in major championships (twenty-three people are logjammed at 63). When the putt horseshoed around the hole and spun out, he scowled, turned away, and tossed his putter aside, clearly exasperated. After the round, he said about the incident, "[I was] mad. I thought I'd made it. It would have been nice to get the record and a three-shot lead going into the weekend. But the important thing is that I hit a good putt . . . it just didn't go in." Seconds after his mini-tantrum, Tiger walked off the green smiling from ear to ear over one of the greatest rounds in the history of tournament golf. It's a big-time, big-business game, but golf is still a game to Tiger. And so is whatever game *you* are playing.

Kids understand this concept naturally. "Kids can play because they're completely present and unaware of themselves," says my friend. "They're focused on what they're doing. Obviously, Tiger does the same, or he'd also be caught up in worrying about the incredible pressure, attention, and expectations that surround his performance. If athletes can be present, they will stop training before the onset of an injury or change strategy if an opponent is getting the better of them or their technique is faltering. But it's the worry about things past and future—'if I skip the workout I'll get fat'—that keeps an athlete going in a negative direction. An athlete, a musician, or any other competitor who knows how to have fun can perform better as a direct consequence." Even an accountant, a receptionist, a toll booth operator, or a prisoner can benefit from injecting some levity into their workday. When Paul Newman's *Cool Hand Luke* character inspired his chain gang to pave a road at record pace, the crew was able to turn even the most miserable labor into a day of singing, laughing, and psychological redemption—the latter by denying the guards their masochistic pleasure of watching the crew suffer physically and emotionally from their toil.

It's OK to Be a Competitor and a Winner

For many, even a simple competition produces emotional distress in the form of pressure, tension, anxiety, and self-esteem attachments to the outcome. Because of these emotional sparks attached to competition, tremendous confusion is present about how to deal with competitive situations in an empowering and graceful manner. A fair portion of the population sprints in the opposite direction away from competition, something that they have grown to loathe in the interest of avoiding judgment and failure. Even with success, society has a perverse tendency to disdain those who achieve it, as evidenced by our lurid revelry in celebrity failures and tribulations. While we are fascinated by the explosion of unfathomable wealth at the top of the food chain, we will mutter comments under our breath that reflect our lack of peace with having less than someone else.

Tiger's "king of the moment" disposition does not in any way conflict with the boat, the mansion, and the proud displays in his trophy room. Putting aside a legitimate discussion on the negative sociopolitical consequences of an inequitable distribution of wealth in modern society, let's admit that money is a resource that is renewable, not scarce. Thousands of people have directly benefited from Tiger's success. The employees of Nike Golf in Beaverton, Oregon (a $500 million a year business, grown from virtually zero before Tiger was signed in 1996); the yacht builders at Christensen Shipyards in Vancouver, Washington; the teachers at the Tiger Woods Learning Center in Anaheim, California; and the construction crews at his estate in Jupiter, Florida, can all feed their families thanks to

Tiger. The fellow PGA Tour players whom Tiger beats up till they go home crying with their tails between their legs are going home with bulging wallets. TV ratings spike 35 to 50 percent when Woods is in contention, according to Sean McManus, president of CBS News and Sports. Tiger's arrival on Tour and exploits from 1997 to 2001 led to $850 million in rights fees for the PGA Tour in 2001 negotiations, a 50 percent increase from pre-Tiger levels. Besides the financial impact, Tiger has inspired professional golfers around the globe (and many other competitors in sports and life) to go for it, pursue their own dreams, and get better. The virtues of trickle-down economics may be highly questionable, but trickle-down inspiration can be enjoyed by all.

Whoever you are and whoever you defeat, you never have to apologize for winning. The great 1960's era long-distance runner Gerry Lindgren described his intriguing and progressive competitive mind-set in his autobiography. "The first step in running well is to know why you are running. Decide that your effort is 100 percent selfless. Determine at the very start that you will run to help others run well. You will be a role model of courage and hard work. You will be the rabbit they work harder to catch. . . . Use your life for a purpose greater than self. Try to use every ounce of your energy to help someone else run faster."

Lindgren continued, "When you live to glorify yourself, energy flows out of you. When you live selflessly for other people, energy flows into you. You can carry a greater load and never get tired. . . . When your running is done unselfishly, for the benefit, happiness and welfare of other people, you tap into a power base other people don't have. Love is power!" Lindgren's "love is power" philosophy is certainly unorthodox and might even seem downright loopy to today's competitor brainwashed by the gladiator mentality, but it is certainly worth examining. Relay split times of elite swimming and track-and-field athletes are consistently faster than their times when competing individually at the same distance. There is no good reason for this except the concept of competing for something bigger than personal glory obviously gives a competitor a quantifiable extra boost. Lindgren and his love power helped revolutionize distance running with his prodigious training volumes and world-class performances while still in high school, and he set a schoolboy five-thousand-meter record that lasted forty years.

Obviously "Tiger Woods" and "selfless performer for the benefit, happiness and welfare of other people" do not match often in word-association games. Tiger wants to kill his opponents and crush their hopes and dreams forever. About the 1997 play-off shot at La Costa, Charles P. Pierce wrote, "I believe that shot was not completely about beating Tom Lehman that afternoon, because Tiger could have used a lemon zester to do that. That shot was for a couple weeks or a year from now, when Lehman is trying to hold a one shot lead over Tiger down the stretch in a major tournament."

When you back up and view the big picture, Lindgren's message becomes more relevant. Golf is the only sport where competitors are so fastidious about the rules that they routinely call penalties on themselves—even when no one would ever know and the lost strokes can take hundreds of thousands of dollars out of their pockets. Tiger unfailingly compliments the good shots of playing partners during rounds, shakes hands or hugs opponents after the round is over, and generally exhibits an incredibly high level of sportsmanship across the board. Even though team playing is hardly his thing—from junior golf to Stanford to the Tour, he has been repeatedly characterized as aloof—Tiger makes a noble effort when it comes time for the Ryder Cup (U.S.A. "all-stars" versus Europe's) and President's Cup (U.S.A. versus international team) competitions. Each competition is held biennially; hence, the top U.S. players annually contest an important team competition. While the media harps on his relatively poor competitive record (as of 2008, his lifetime combined record from both events is under .500) as a testament to Tiger's self-centeredness, his teammates—the more astute observers by a landslide—universally laud him for his exemplary and infectious competitive intensity.

It really is no problem for sportsmanship and competitiveness to coexist, as Tida advocated in her now-classic admonition to step on some throats during battle. Surely you have encountered folks who seem truly dedicated to helping others and still come out ahead. Once, in keeping with my adolescent behavior tendencies, I placed a crank call to my friend Bob Powers, who runs a large wholesale electrical supply business in Sacramento, California. When he took the call from his flustered assistant, I immediately launched into an angry hysterical tirade (in one of my extremely convincing, indistinguishably multiethnic accents) about my fictitious order going awry. He responded immediately with calmness and sincerity, "OK, slow down, slow down. Let's sort this out together. Let's get to the bottom of this issue and solve it!" I laid it on even thicker in an effort to crack him, to no avail. I closed the conversation by having him discover with me that I'd dialed the wrong company, to which he said, "Well, give me a call if we can ever serve you at Granite Electric."

When a busy leader deals with a total dorkhead with patience, grace, and a big-picture perspective, you obtain an outstanding character-revealing insight. Wouldn't you want to do business with someone like that? Indeed, Powers has presided over a smashing success in the past several years. His relatively new business has decimated larger, more established competitors by being good to employees (attracting droves of top talent from rival firms) and fostering goodwill with suppliers and customers through frequent premium golf and salmon fishing junkets. Powers tour guides these junkets so he can form meaningful friendships with people in his world by sharing the exhilaration of hitting greens and reeling in big fish. As with Google and other progressive companies, he experiences an enjoyable by-product—the correlation between his enlightened mind-set and his firm's annual revenues.

Working Smart

Golf instructor Hank Haney has received much notoriety as Tiger's swing coach and orchestrator of the new and improved swing that made its magnificent debut in 2005. Their relationship offers an interesting glimpse of the importance of having quality instruction and guidance to ensure that hard work doesn't go to waste. As Haney said in a 2005 *Golf Digest* article titled "Tips for Your Game," "Improve the quality of your practice. No more blind experimenting, hoping you'll stumble upon a secret or sensation that will become permanent. Get with your pro and make a list of three clear objectives. Give them time to sink in, and you will improve."

Haney discussed his role with Tiger in an interview at the 2007 British Open. "I walk with [Tiger] the whole time. I talk to him, give him input. He'll run ideas by me, things he thinks he'll do on the course, or what clubs he's going to play off the tees. Primarily, I'm just there to observe his swing and answer any questions he has and to make sure he's hitting the ball like he was last week in practice." Again, we have to stretch our imagination a little to apply the lesson to our own circumstances. It might not make sense (or dollars) for you to hire a private instructor to follow you during golf rounds, nor a life coach to rap with for twenty minutes each morning to get you pumped for your workday. But many can benefit from making a more devoted effort to seek help from experts and establish smart work habits.

Learning that Tiger has some dude following him around charting his shots might not be big news, but it's revealing that few other touring pros have a similar arrangement in place. These guys who make millions of dollars per year and are desperate to take down Tiger nevertheless fall short, for whatever reason, of enlisting as much help and support as Tiger does. Annika Sorenstam, arguably the greatest female golfer in history, enjoys engaging in detailed scientific analysis of her competitive rounds. For decades, she has entered each shot into a spreadsheet to determine error patterns (missed left, missed right, and so forth) and then addresses these specific and clearly identified weaknesses in practice. She has also famously transformed her physique to become one of the strongest and longest-hitting women on Tour—previously a weak area for her. It's typical at the very top of the ladder to find stories like these, leading one to wonder if the chicken (champion athlete) or the egg (ethic for smart, hard, fun work) came first.

Once upon a time, Annika and Tiger made an initial foray into the unknown—their local fitness facility—in their quest to improve their golf games through strength training. They were focused ruthlessly on improving their weaknesses, open-minded to embrace the expertise of others, and willing to swallow their pride and accept that, while they ruled on the golf course, they were novices in the gym. Believe it or not, these qualities can be considered rare among peak performers. The stereotypical modern elite athletes (or business leaders)—macho, cocky, self-absorbed, all-knowing—will have some or much resistance to dismantling their success formula and reaching out to experts who can help them get to the next level—it's too risky for their massive egos.

At Stanford, Tiger balanced the scale at 6'1", 158 pounds, and earned extra spending money posing as a stick figure for Stanford's art students. Not really, but he has certainly put in a tremendous amount of work to produce today's ripped 185-pound, 9 percent body-fat physique. A *Men's Fitness* cover story mentions that "[Tiger's] routine is built around stretching up to 40 minutes before each session, core exercises, endurance runs of seven miles and speed runs of three miles, along with weight training. Tiger's trainer Keith Kleven says, 'Pound for pound, I put him with any athlete in the world.'"

Aligning Behavior with Stated Goals

According to the National Golf Foundation, the 25.6 million regular golfers in the United States shoot an average score of 100 for eighteen holes (97 for men, 114 for women). Only 6 percent of men and 1 percent of women break 80 regularly. Despite dramatic advances in clubs, ball performance, and course grooming over the past couple decades, the average score has remained consistent. If greater interest in peak performance were generated among the masses and our twenty-five million golfers took more lessons and spent more time practicing, the average golf score would dip sharply. Similarly, ironman triathletes exhibit a phenomenal work ethic, balancing busy careers and personal lives with hours of grueling workouts in each sport. These high-energy type-A's have no problem setting the alarm for 5:30 A.M. to jump into the water for a swim workout. However, an extremely small percentage of them take regular swim lessons, a critical factor for improvement in such a technique-dependent sport. Without intensive instruction, someone who swims frequently—or hits golf shots frequently—is ingraining into the nervous system technique flaws that become that much harder to correct. A simple thirty-minute lesson with video analysis can result in more improvement than hours and hours of practicing poor mechanics, yet there is resistance to taking the sensible, time-efficient route.

All that said, it's important to understand that it's OK if you are committed to something short of elite-level peak performance. Maybe a swim workout or a golf round is a chance to get a refreshing break from the pressures of real life and enjoy some quality time with friends, technique flaws be darned. One of my favorite golf partners will typically play seriously for twelve to fourteen holes and then, if his accumulated score is unsatisfactory, degenerate in the homestretch with goofy shots and practical jokes. The silliness makes me realize that golf is just a game and helps me appreciate the big picture of enjoying friends, nature, free time, and having fun as the ultimate goal. In college one of my main objectives at library study sessions was to make my future wife and her friends laugh and get us kicked out of the quiet rooms. We can still laugh about it twenty-five years later. If a fulfilling part of your workday is to instant message your buddies, share funny YouTube links, and chat in the break room in between trying to meet your objectives, there is no inherent harm in that (well, your boss might disagree; if so, buy her a copy of *How Tiger Does It* for Christmas).

The harmless stuff only becomes harmful when you talk out one side of your mouth and live incongruently with your spouted ideals. If you want to pursue peak performance as a golfer or triathlete or in the workplace, you have to make the requisite commitments and sacrifices. Swimmers best implement technique changes at slow speeds, which dims their sense of accomplishment and exhilaration at any single workout. Golfers—even Tiger—will struggle to perform in the short term while they try to implement technique corrections from the lesson tee. Focusing on a promotion and increased productivity in the workplace might mean moving on from your current posse of cool coworkers to associate with a stiffer crew and cutting out the superfluous elements of your workday. If you say you are angling for a promotion but you can't delete those jokes from your in-box or pull away from watercooler gossip, then you are creating harm and confusion to your psyche by living incongruently with your stated purpose.

As Tiger Woods models, you can still have fun and pursue peak performance, but you must establish clear boundaries and balance intense focus with relaxation. For your day on the golf course, you can compete intently until the last putt drops on the eighteenth hole, adjourn to the clubhouse for refreshments, then head back out at twilight, barefoot with a couple clubs and engage in high jinks and hazing with your playing partners. You can maintain your focus during the workday proper and then let it all hang out with coworkers during happy hour. Clear and focused transitions are more productive and less stressful than when you blur the lines like that character in the library. Be honest with yourself and ask where your true goals and motivations lay. You do not owe it to the world to break 80 or get a promotion. Being a good person and leaving an honorable legacy extends far beyond the bullet points on your curriculum vitae. However, if you are going to show up at work for a couple thousand hours each year and devote free time, energy, and passion to your hobbies, why not challenge yourself to be as strategic and successful as possible?

BEING A GOOD PERSON AND LEAVING AN HONORABLE LEGACY EXTENDS FAR BEYOND THE BULLET POINTS ON YOUR CURRICULUM VITAE.

At the youth soccer practices I coach, I conduct kids versus parents scrimmages to show the kids the importance of staying in position on the field—something the young age groups struggle with. A couple parents will launch crisp passes back and forth, twenty yards apart, while the kids leave their positions to chase the ball in both directions until they are ragged. Then we pause and discuss the possibility of everyone staying in position, waiting to defend a possible return pass to their area. The kids have fun screaming and giggling while we wear them out playing keep away, but working smart is even more fun. They experience a breakthrough in skills and strategy by staying in position and working more effectively as a team. Similarly, breaking 100, 90, or 80 can be an even bigger rush than farting at the perfect time to crack up your partner in midbackswing.

Improving Through Coaching and Self-Reflection

In athletics, it's very clear why and how one must engage in practice that translates directly into better competitive performance. If you miss short putts during the round, go practice short putts on the green until you become comfortable with them. If you keep double faulting in tennis matches, get some lessons to improve your technique and smash dozens of serves against a backboard so you can do the same in a match.

In the office, the classroom, or other endeavors, things are often less clear-cut. How can the student improve from a B average to an A average? How can you prevail over other wannabes for the promotion? An entire range of work and lifestyle habits must be examined to determine how the weaknesses are showing up in the competitive arena and how to counteract them. To discover and overcome your weaknesses, you have to be brutally honest with yourself, instead of rationalizing away behavior that compromises performance or ignores blind spots.

Today, however, it is easy to avoid the mirror or the starting line. Instead, you can aspire to and revel in the achievement of super dilettante status: someone with substantial intellect who is well educated, well read, passionate, and opinionated about a great many topics, possesses excellent communication and persuasion skills, enjoys a diverse network of friends, and even generates a good income—but who contributes or creates virtually nothing, takes no risks, and qualifies as one of Teddy Roosevelt's "poor spirits who live in the gray twilight that knows neither victory nor defeat." People have made careers out of responding and reacting to e-mails and instant messages, showing up, looking good, and speaking the lingo in meetings and conference calls, brainstorming strategy and theory ad nauseam and "managing" people, projects, and processes— while others do most all of the actual work. It pays pretty well if you can play the game right and are not chapped by selling pieces of your soul along the way.

OK, so you claim to be a playah in the fast lane, not a poor spirit in the gray twilight. It's still not easy to be honest with yourself or notice your shortcomings when you are completely wrapped up in your endeavors. In the final stages of my nine-year professional triathlon career, I suffered a steady decline in results. Though it was clearly time to step away, I found it difficult to face and deal with that reality after nine years of total focus on swim, bike, and run. My friend Peter Coulson, husband and coach of the greatest female triathlete in history, Australian Michelle Jones, was instrumental in my facing and accepting the reality that I was not able to compete at a top level anymore nor was I even truly interested in doing so. While I was doing the song and dance with sponsors and myself about "encouraging" workouts and race results in my quest to return to top form, Coulson would phone me and unload in his brusque Aussie accent. "Kearns, you suck. Fourth place sucks. Look who beat you; those guys suck. I remember when you could get off the bike and run away from everyone, like at Orange County in '91. Now look at you. You should f—ing retire, Kearns." The caustic style was just what I needed to penetrate through the facade of eternal optimism and unbreakable self-confidence that athletes must manufacture to compete at the elite level. Even a victory would be met by Coulson with, "Oh yeah, who was second? He sucks, he's a nobody. Third? Never heard of him. You beat no one. That was a nothing race—a cherry pick. It's time to retire."

Do you have someone looking over your shoulder, telling it like it is? Or are you surrounded by a bunch of sycophants, politically correct safe distance–keeping coworkers and super dilettante friends, who see your blind spots and know the truth but, for whatever reason (social custom, don't care enough, noses too upturned, or fear of repercussion), don't bother opening up to you? This is especially relevant the higher up the competitive ladder you climb. Even—or especially—if you are a CEO or world champion, you have to seek out unfiltered critical feedback, hone your listening skills, and be open to self-reflection and adaptation.

Tiger is a master of organizing, inspiring, and leading a winning team of players intensely devoted to peak performance; it's a prerequisite for joining and staying on his team. He is also a master of self-reflection and successfully implementing the constructive critique of others. After his March 2007 victory at the World Golf Championship's (a series of big-money, invite field events) CA Championship at Doral in Miami, Tiger was asked about his penchant for winning on the heels of disappointing play the previous week. To that date, on twenty-three occasions where he finished a tournament out of the top twenty, he'd come back the next week and won thirteen times. The "amazing Tiger stat" file is getting pretty full, but that one's definitely cool. "I think you have to analyze your performance and where you went wrong. Too many people are afraid to look deep down and look at where you made mistakes. That's not always easy to do, to be honest with yourself. That's something my father always instilled in me and even to this day, sometimes it's difficult, but you have to take an honest look and have an honest evaluation of your performance."

EVEN—OR ESPECIALLY—IF YOU ARE A CEO OR WORLD CHAMPION, YOU HAVE TO SEEK OUT UNFILTERED CRITICAL FEEDBACK, HONE YOUR LISTENING SKILLS, AND BE OPEN TO SELF-REFLECTION AND ADAPTATION.

Back to Tiger's decision to retool his swing in 1997. Think of the circumstances—a twenty-one-year-old kid suddenly at the very top of the sporting world, inking multimillion-dollar deals left and right and reducing the Masters into a pitch-and-putt exhibition (at the '97 tournament, he never hit more than a seven-iron into any par-4 and hit eight- and nine-irons into the storied par-5 thirteenth and fifteenth holes on the back nine). Floating on cloud nine, fresh off an abbreviated vacation in Cancun (Tigermania had already spread there and he couldn't relax in public), he chose that time to critically review videotape and decide to dismantle the vehicle that won him the Indy 500.

"SOMETIMES IT'S DIFFICULT, BUT YOU HAVE TO TAKE AN HONEST LOOK AND HAVE AN HONEST EVALUATION OF YOUR PERFORMANCE."

—Tiger Woods

We can certainly do the same under less dramatic circumstances. If the BlackBerry is chirping and chipping away at family time or your exuberance in meetings is suppressing valuable input from someone with a softer voice, step back for a moment and reflect. Can you be a better leader by empowering others to share center stage and be the best they can be? Is there a better way to balance your career with your life that can lead to more fulfillment and pro-ductivity and less stress? Can you still have fun if you get a little more focused about school, sports, or work and cut out or strictly compartmentalize the fluff? The answer across the board is quite likely yes, as we see from the best golfer in the world, who knows that "there's always stuff to work on. You never, ever arrive. But it sure is fun trying."

TIPS FOR CULTIVATING A
STRONG WORK-PLAY ETHIC

1. Make work fun. It's not enough anymore to simply put your head down, work hard, and produce results. Reject the "just make it through the day" mentality rooted in narrow values such as puritanical social climbing. The most powerful competitive stance is to get the biggest rush from the battle itself. By releasing your attachment to the outcome, you can experience the pure joy of competition and push your limits without distraction in pursuit of peak performance. Cultivate a pure motivation that extends beyond winning and losing, as Tiger demonstrated when he overhauled his swing despite competitive success. Pursue endeavors that you love and that represent the highest expression of your talents. Have fun at all costs, understanding that this is the true secret of champions.

2. Expand your horizons. Discard society's harmful programming that values shortcuts, decadence, and conformity. Forget moderation in this context—take risks and push limits to realize true peak performance. Transcend the energy struggle to beat opponents and the repetition of control dramas that you developed as coping mechanisms throughout your life. Realize that pursuing something bigger than your selfish needs will lead to performance breakthroughs thanks to the "love is power" concept. A selfless, evolved approach will create a collective escalation of passion among those around you and provide a more powerful, pure, and long-lasting source of motivation than focusing narrowly on personal gain.

continued

3. Be comfortable with competition. The negative emotional baggage connected with results-oriented competitiveness has led many to loathe putting it all on the line due to fear of failure. Winners contribute to the peak performance and personal growth of all competitors, so don't be afraid to enjoy victory and the yachts and mansions that you might accumulate as a consequence. Become comfortable "going for the throat in competition, then sportsmanship after." If you're seven shots back with seven holes to play, don't give up; relish the opportunity to chase. If you are ahead or running neck and neck with a competitor, savor the opportunity to push each other to greater heights.

4. Work smart. Having fun and working hard will not lead to success unless your work is focused, guided by expert coaching, and directly applicable to your peak performance goals. Be brutally honest with yourself and make a clear decision to align your behavior with your stated goal of peak performance. Understand that this entails sacrificing things that bring you and your ego a certain measure of satisfaction but will lead to more fulfillment and productivity and less stress. Pay particular attention to the importance of focusing on one endeavor at a time and achieving a smooth transition to the next. Seek out coaches, experts, and friends who will tell it like it is. Do the same when you look into the mirror, and then take specific and decisive action to address your weaknesses. Witness the example of scrawny Tiger and Annika venturing into the weight room and emerging with another distinct advantage over their rivals.

5. Share the secret. Realize that most people are trapped in an existence of self-importance, consumerism, hectic pace, and high stress levels. By taking a stand for the importance of play, fun, and enjoyment of the moment, you serve as a powerful role model to wake up others and connect them with their childlike inner spirit. After following Tiger around the golf course during a 2007 tournament, I couldn't help but contrast his effortless swing tempo, relaxed pace, total focus, and baseline state of complete tranquility with the powerful emotional reactions I had during my own round of golf the following day. Similarly, encountering a happy, energetic person can lighten your mood in an instant. By taking risks in difficult relationships by communicating, rejecting controlling dramas, and looking beyond self-interest to try and give more, you can help others arise from their dreams and coax them out of their ruts. Sure, no one is immune to the trials and tribulations of life, but everyone deserves to enjoy some fun in the pursuit of peak performance.

5

TIGER SUCCESS FACTOR 3
BALANCED APPROACH

As we discussed in Chapter 1, Tiger's unique, process-oriented, balanced approach represents an evolution of the ultimate peak performer mentality that is destined to become the norm in the future. A balanced approach is applicable on a few different levels. In the physical dimension, it's critical to balance hard work with rest and relaxation. The physically balanced athlete can avoid pitfalls such as injury, burnout, and flagging motivation levels that occur when natural laws are ignored in favor of the ego-driven accumulation of work and results. You must balance competitive intensity with a detachment to the outcome, and you must also strive for a balanced life perspective—a spiritual balance. As we learned from Bannister and Lindgren, a performer motivated by the indomitable human spirit and the power of love—love of competition and the process of pursuing peak performance—can keep going when others motivated solely by trophy, glory, or money will quit, choke, or get distracted or discouraged by these superficial and imbalanced motivators.

Being balanced in the broad sense will foster pure and sustained high motivation levels and help keep a performer grounded in the face of both failure and success—providing a distinct advantage over the self-absorbed, one-dimensional performer competing with others for energy and results. At a press conference for the 2005 Tiger-hosted Target World Challenge tournament in Thousand Oaks, California, Tiger talked about the importance of balance in his career. "You don't want to have one thing dominate your life, which when I first came out here, that's what it was, nothing but golf. It had to be; I had to get my career started. But as I got closer to O'Meara and being around him, he made me pointedly aware of how important it is to have balance. If you want to survive out here for a long period of time you have to have balance, you have to have outlets. That's when I started getting other hobbies. He took me on a bunch of fishing trips. And now I've kind of gone away from the fishing that he does, fly fishing, I've gone to spear fishing. Obviously my personal life has changed by being married. It's been fantastic for me to have that balance, it's tough playing out here all the time with all the things and distractions and pressures you have to deal with. But it's nice to have other outlets to get away."

Physical Balance: Stress + Rest = Adaptation

The principle of stress + rest = adaptation is one of the natural laws of the universe and critical to the continued improvement in any endeavor, but particularly athletic pursuits. Unfortunately, many driven peak performers ignore this common sense in favor of accumulating more and more work. Forcing improvement to happen unnaturally generates guaranteed side effects such as injury, illness, burnout, or regression in performance.

The true definition of *stress* is any form of stimulation to the mind or body. Stress is a natural and healthy component of life. The only way to learn and excel in any endeavor is to stress yourself and experience an adaptation as a result. To be stress-free equates with boredom or literally death. Our typical use of the term *stress* conveys a condition of *distress* or overstimulation. A quick overview of the fight-or-flight response will confirm this. When you encounter significant stress—external stimulation—your adrenal glands release hormones into your bloodstream that allow the body to function at a heightened level. With this "adrenalin rush," heart rate, blood pressure, and breathing rate increase and senses become more acute. This mechanism, perfected into our genes over thousands of years as a survival necessity, is a great help if you are in a track meet or facing a life-threatening situation. Not so if your stress is a traffic jam, an argument, or a competitive round of golf (where physical demands are minimal and relaxation—the opposite of the fight-or-flight response—is critical).

Today the fight-or-flight response is severely abused as we live in a world where stimulation is unrelenting. In response to the fast-moving, multitasking, technologically overwhelming, crowded, polluted, materialistic modern world, we become hyperaroused for sustained periods of time without adequate rest. Eventually, the coping mechanism becomes exhausted and your adrenals start releasing less than normal amounts of these hormones that are crucial to health and peak function. This condition, best described as burnout, has symptoms such as recurring fatigue, sugar cravings, energy level swings, digestive problems, muscle and joint pain, nervousness, irritability, emotional instability, and a weakened immune system. Over the long haul, the condition of sustained overstress is believed to be the leading risk factor for lifestyle-related diseases such as heart disease and many cancers.

There are many ways to arrive at that place called burnout. You can get it through intense physical training; working long hours; traveling extensively; eating poorly; consuming too much alcohol, coffee, sugar, or other junk food; or dealing with family difficulties such as a separation, an extended illness, or a personal tragedy. The simplest and most powerful cure and prevention strategy against burnout is to integrate regular, planned downtime into your lifestyle. If you can't discipline yourself to do this, downtime will be offered to you in the form of illness or exhaustion.

Often you become so conditioned to your daily routine and lifestyle circumstances that you aren't even aware of how stressful your life is. This is particularly true when you consider that many forms of stress in your daily routine happen to be enjoyable. You also often hear the literal misnomer that exercise is a great stress release from the pressures of a busy workday and family life. While it can be a great emotional and mental outlet to balance other forms of stress, it is essential to remember that exercise is merely a different form of stress. Your body's stress response is identical regardless of whether you consider the stimulation enjoyable or upsetting. The trick is to moderate your behavior so you can thrive on the positive effects of the various forms of stress in your life and minimize the negative effects of too much stress.

Tiger may be quite comfortable with his status and destiny to be the world's greatest and best-known athlete, but it makes for an incredibly stimulating—that is, stressful—life. Privacy is nonexistent, attention and exposure are enormous, and his competitive environment is extremely intense. From the moment he leaves his home to travel to a tournament to the time he returns home, Tiger is subjected to virtually unrelenting stress in many forms—jet travel, endless media and public attention, and, of course, the challenge of shooting a low score in professional competition. I believe Tiger's reporting of frequent colds and allergies to grass, trees, and pollen is exacerbated by this repeated exposure to high-stress tournament golf. Consequently, Tiger must be extremely sensitive and proactive about managing his competitive and life stress effectively and preserve physical, mental, and emotional health. His efforts are evident in the fact that—despite massive financial incentives to play more frequently—he has entered an average of only nineteen tournaments per year in his career, versus the typical range of twenty-five to thirty-five among PGA Tour pros.

While Tiger reveals little of his behind-the-scenes training habits, it's been reported by the *New York Times* and the *Wall Street Journal* that he practices Pilates and even qigong (an ancient Chinese practice similar to yoga, focused on energy restoration and flexibility). He's mentioned his interest in spear fishing (maybe that's why he bought his "boat") as well as skiing. At the 2006 Target World Challenge press conference, he was asked, "Are you a black diamond skier these days—black diamond, the hardest?" "It's not the hardest," Tiger responded. "Double black?" "Mm hmm," answered Tiger, generating laughter in the audience.

"WHEN I'M OFF THE GOLF COURSE, I LIKE TO GET AWAY FROM EVERYTHING, AND I LIKE TO KEEP EVERYTHING PRIVATE, BECAUSE I FEEL I HAVE A RIGHT TO DO THAT."

—Tiger Woods

It's a safe bet that Tiger gorges on other purely restorative activities to balance his time in the spotlight and his exhausting schedule of golf practice and competitions. Let's leave it at that and figure out for our own what restores and rejuvenates our energy. As David Owen related in his book *The Chosen One*, Tiger was once asked by a young fan at a golf clinic how he balances golf and personal life. "When I'm off the golf course, I like to get away from everything, and I like to keep everything private, because I feel I have a right to do that. I have a right to my own private life, and the things I like to do."

Understanding the Stress-Rest Balance in the Big Picture

It's clear that peak performance requires high energy, total concentration, and thus frequent breaks and balancing efforts. It's also clear that this principle is habitually ignored by most competitive athletes, corporate hard drivers, and harried multitasking moms. Even young people are socialized to disrespect the importance of adequate sleep, nutrition, and physical exercise and of the enjoyment of nature in favor of overscheduled routines and digital entertainment.

Tiger's sizzling 2006 season was highlighted by his winning the season's last two majors—British Open and PGA—and the final six tournaments he entered. The years of hard work to groove his swing are finally clicking, he's on one of the hottest streaks in the history of golf, and what does he do? As he told the press conference audience at the January 2006 season-opening Buick Invitational in San Diego, "I took some time off. I didn't touch a club for twenty-four days, which is the longest I've ever gone, I think, ever. Yeah, I didn't touch a club. Normally I would say I didn't swing a club for twenty-four days, but I would be monkeying around with it at home. But I decided this time that I should get away from the game completely and come back recharged. . . . I had some new knickknack things [minor injuries] that I was trying to play through in the last year, and was just really tired toward the end of last year, too, and just mentally trying to play that many events overseas and come back and play, it wore me out a little bit. Also my ankle wasn't doing too good and I had a little bit of a shoulder deal. You make up for one thing and all of a sudden something else acts up, and that's what happened. So I had to lay low and let everything heal. [During the break] I didn't do much of anything. I just hung around the house and just really chilled and just laid low."

Taking twenty-four consecutive days off work and the rest of your life responsibilities or pursuing extravagant getaway hobbies might be out of reach for most of us, but we can apply the principle of balancing stress and rest on many different levels. For the nine-to-fiver faced with a hundred phone calls or seventy-eight delivery stops, five days a week all year long except for those precious two weeks of American vacation time, unplugging might seem like a foreign concept. However, we can and must always maximize whatever balancers we can make available. Getting adequate sleep each night, eating a nutritious, natural-foods diet, avoiding unhealthy vices, addictions, and relationships, enjoying a weekend away from the intensive schedules and responsibilities of the work or school week, and taking a proper lunch hour to escape physically and mentally from the work environment are critical components of peak performance, general good health and fitness, and overall happiness and well-being.

Understanding that stress really means *stimulation*, your quest for balance must consider stimulating diversions such as physical exercise, golf rounds, social gatherings, even watching an action DVD with surround sound, in the same category as work, traffic jams, emotional distress, and paying the bills. On the other side of the equation are things such as sleep, meditation, yoga, quiet reading, a stroll through the neighborhood, and bird-watching. That doesn't mean you must refrain from cardio workouts, golf, skiing, or spear fishing on your time away from the office. Just remember the big-picture view and the importance of true rest to remain in balance.

Promoting Spontaneous, Intuitive Improvement

The concept of stress and rest is directly relevant to the truth that performance improvement usually happens in a spontaneous manner and almost never in a linear manner. When children learn to read or do math, they don't improve their skills 2 percent every day for six months. As brain researcher Jane Healy explains in detail in *Your Child's Growing Mind*, the learning process is one of spontaneous breakthroughs. One day kids suddenly get it and spring to the next level of ability and cognition. Athletes can surely relate, as often months and months of hard training include performance plateaus or even regressions. Then one day things just click and they amaze themselves with a new personal-best performance.

Whether your goal is lowering your weight or your golf score or raising your tax bracket, your actions should not be governed by a cookie-cutter template but by your intuitive sense of what is the right thing to do on a daily, weekly, monthly, and annual basis. I define *intuition* as a blend of instinct; critical thinking and reasoning; common sense; awareness of mental, physical, and emotional states; and an ability to see the big picture of your life and your competitive goals.

The opposite of the intuitive approach is an obsessive-compulsive approach, where ego demands and other negative influences create a disconnect between mind and body. If you doggedly pursue material success, brazenly sacrificing your health, your family, and a balanced life to work longer and harder than the competition, you will most likely succeed by rat-race standards. However, when your performance goals include the desire to be healthy and happy, or involve your physical body, applying a linear, obsessive mentality will likely result in emotional distress and physical exhaustion. If this were not the case, some dude of limited intellectual means could go to the driving range, hit balls for fifteen hours a day, and supplant Tiger Woods as the world's best golfer.

It's admittedly tough to downshift from the Type-A mentality we've been conditioned to adopt for success and cultivate our intuition, but we all have the ability—it's wired into our basic nature as human beings. When we get tired at night, we lay our heads on a pillow and go to sleep. We don't need to hire a personal sleeping trainer to keep us motivated—it's a natural inclination and a good example of intuition at work. Even simple behaviors such as yawning (an attempt to increase energy levels by inhaling deeply), sighing (an attempt to relax with an extended exhale), or going to the restroom are good examples of a strong mind-body connection and intuitive decision making.

As we mentioned earlier, we see mostly the overt elements of Tiger's athletic prowess—the incredible physical power of his shots and the fist-pumping competitive intensity. What's harder to notice are the subtle and intuitive factors at work. Tiger practices for hours on end back home in Florida between tournaments, but unlike the obsessive competitor, his sessions are purposeful and always aligned with his energy level, motivation level, and health. Tiger knows exactly the right time to take a break—at each practice session, when committing to tournaments over the course of the year, and when shutting it down in the off-season. This is a difficult skill to master, for the carefully cultivated mind-set of the competitive athlete is to never give up, give in, or give a hoot about fluffy concepts such as balance.

Tiger mentioned the importance of restraint in regard to his devoted strength-training regimen. "I've never, ever hurt myself lifting. I hear people say, 'I hurt this' or 'I hurt that.' I don't even know what that feels like. I've been sore, but I've always been able to function and do whatever I wanted to. Some people let their ego get in the way. You have to listen to your inner self. Your body knows when it can be pushed and when you just need to back off a little bit."

However, the bulletproof mind-set is valuable in the heat of battle, when forces conspire to try and break your competitive spirit and make you quit. After the 2003 Bay Hill Tournament in Orlando, Florida, where a weather delay required Tiger to play twenty-nine holes in a single day, Tiger was asked if he was bothered by the long day. "I think that's when it helps to be in decent shape. You're going to get tired, yeah, but it's a matter of . . . understanding that you're fatigued, but your body is still firing, you can still hit golf shots. Just because you're tired doesn't mean you are going to hit bad golf shots. I think that's where what I've been doing off the golf course [his fitness regimen] really helps." Flip back to Sergio for a moment and his bellyaching about his fifteen-minute delay on the final hole of the British Open. Do you have examples in your own life where you complained too much about your competitive circumstances and suffered accordingly? How about a time when you went with the flow and prospered while others around you complained and suffered?

The ironman mind-set in competition must be carefully balanced with an opposing mind-set in the big picture of everyday life and the pursuit of long-term goals—one that is sensitive and intuitive. This enables a highly competitive athlete to avoid injury, burnout, and declining performance brought about by doing too much at the wrong time. The Tiger oblivious to on-course fatigue is also famous for his great escapes from the spotlight to chill and lay low. During his 1997 season when Tiger hysteria, and consequently the stress of being Tiger, was at full strength, he had this to say about an upcoming break on the heels of five tournaments in six weeks: "I'm going to be relaxing. I'm not going to pick up a club for a while. I've had enough golf for a bit. And I'm going to get my mind squared away and get my focus back. I need a lot of rest dealing with all this [the intensive media and fan attention at every tournament]. It's hard. . . . I run myself in the ground."

The cultural pressure to forget about this touchy-feely stuff is substantial and the fallout is tremendous. Bookstore shelves are lined with material addressing the challenges of today's hectic, stressful world for harried moms, business executives, and youths. An August 2007 *New York Times* article about working millionaires in Silicon Valley contained some choice quotes revealing the distorted mind-sets of the affluent surrounded by the superrich. "Everyone around here looks at the people above them. You're nobody here at $10 million [net worth]," said one. "The pressures to spend more are everywhere," said another. "You see how much money you have in the bank, and your eyes get really big [as you upsize] your life to your cash flow," said another. Hence, they work twelve-hour days trying to get ahead in an environment one calls "the Silicon Valley salt mines." Madeline Levine's *Price of Privilege* explains how affluent children suffer from high parental expectations to achieve, exhausting schedules, and materialism replacing quality family time. The result is large numbers of kids who are dispassionate, disconnected, and suffering from alarming rates of depression, anxiety disorders, and substance abuse.

We even have difficulty respecting athletes who strive to balance competitive intensity with time off. When Tiger steps off the Tour to restore his energy, the media lights into him, TV executives grimace, and the affected Tour stops are devastated. In the 1984 Olympics, Carl Lewis was resoundingly booed by ninety thousand fans while he won a gold medal in the long jump—one of his four golds at the Los Angeles games, matching the legendary achievement of Jesse Owens in 1936. You see, Lewis only took two jumps and then passed on his remaining allotted four because his twenty-eight-foot mark—the fourth-longest jump in history—was far superior to the next closest competitor and he needed to conserve energy for his remaining events (100 meters, 200 meters, and 4 × 100 meter relay). The myopic ticket holders who pay good money to see these amazing feats want it all: six jumps, four golds, and not too far of a walk from the parking lot to their seat.

Balancing Yin and Yang to Win

The basis of Eastern spiritual practices such as Taoism and traditional Chinese medicine is the concept of yin and yang. This unity-of-opposites theory suggests that all forms of energy on earth must move in harmony with opposing forms to sustain optimum life. These opposing forces (yin and yang) are everywhere, particularly in nature. Hence, the Chinese medical tenet that wood, fire, earth, metal, and water represent the basic phases of the material world; each is represented in our physical bodies and must remain in balance for optimum health and performance. For example, a fever (or excess heat and perspiration) could indicate an imbalance of fire and a need to nourish water. You can also apply the opposing-forces concept—the traditional yang energy (light, masculine, active) with traditional yin (dark, feminine, passive)—to our discussion about balancing stress and rest, the quest for results, and the appreciation of the process.

Robert Wright's 2000 *Slate Magazine* article titled "Gandhi and Tiger Woods" pursued the spiritual-balance theme in connection with Tiger's exploits.

> To be a great golfer, you have to do what some Eastern religions stress—live in the present and free yourself of aspiration and anxiety. You can't be angry over a previous error or worried about repeating it, nor can you be dreaming of future glory. Gandhi used to say he tried to strive on "without fear of failure and without hope of success." . . . [Tiger] has talked often about the importance of "staying in the present" and not letting your mind wander to the victory putt on the 18th hole.
>
> There is another dimension of present-mindedness and another sense in which some great golfers go beyond the merely "mental." In fact, they even achieve a kind of triumph over thought. Though thinking is vital to hole-by-hole strategizing and the year-round honing of your swing, when the moment comes to actually execute your swing, conscious thought is the enemy of success. At the moment of impact, various golf philosophers have held, your mind should be empty—you should be focused on the task at hand in a kind of [nonverbal] way. Many golfers are good at this sort of unconscious concentration, but the utter consistency with which Tiger Woods seems to achieve it almost does qualify him as supernatural. This paradox—that utter present-mindedness

involves a kind of willful mindlessness—is of course quite Eastern. In Zen meditation, one object of the game is to empty your mind of thought.

Tiger offered some thoughts on the subject to David Owen for his *Men's Vogue* article. "I will never say that I have telekinesis. But I do think that when I am in that moment when my concentration is the highest, when it's at its peak, I see things more clearly, and things happen slower. And I think they happen easier. When that moment happens, it's like it's magic. I wish I could be down the stretch in a major championship every week, because it's the calmest I ever feel."

"I WISH I COULD BE DOWN THE STRETCH IN A MAJOR CHAMPIONSHIP EVERY WEEK, BECAUSE IT'S THE CALMEST I EVER FEEL."

—Tiger Woods

Granted, learning that Tiger can enter the magic zone where everything slows down for him and his completely calm self helps for shit during your own round. However, we all have this ability to be completely present and in fact experience it often. Unfortunately, it typically happens by chance, when we least expect it, when ideal mental and environmental conditions conspire to help us relax and connect mind and body. Afterward, we reflect on how great the experience was and express a desire to control the process and enter the zone at will. In the mere act of analyzing the flow, we disconnect from its magic, an unfortunate catch-22. Maybe you are tossing stones at tree trunks during a peaceful hike along a forest trail and notice that, by golly, you've hit the target seven times in a row. Perhaps that's impressive enough to remark enthusiastically to your companions, setting the stage for the next attempt, with all eyes watching as you hit nothing but air.

It would be useful to purposefully create some competitive circumstances that help you disengage the overanalytical mind and connect with the present. The fascinating sport of speed golf (also called extreme golf) is an ideal activity to facilitate this process. In speed golf, players try to play the course as quickly as possible on foot (some tournaments allow caddies driving carts to supply the clubs, or a player will carry a junior bag with an abbreviated set). A player's speed golf score is a combination of total strokes and total minutes spent on the course. World record holder Jay Larson (a remarkable athlete whose résumé includes a scratch handicap and PGA golf pro license, a stint as a tennis professional, an eleventh-place finish in the 1987 Hawaii Ironman as a pro triathlete, and also time in the minor leagues of professional baseball) once shot a 71 on a regulation-length course (six thousand yards or more) in thirty-seven minutes, producing a total speed golf score of 108. Professional golfer Chris Smith once shot a 65 in forty-four minutes at a 2005 Chicago tournament for a 109 total.

The most remarkable phenomenon in tournament or casual play is that nearly every participant shoots as good as or better than their regular score, despite rushing around the course and eschewing the traditional deliberate preparation in favor of taking a deep breath and whacking a shot immediately. It seems the lack of tension or overanalysis results in free swings and putts that stay on target. In my tournament appearances, I was absolutely shocked when I'd step up to a long putt, chest heaving and arms trembling from the effort of sprinting in from the fairway, quickly glance at the line, and stroke the ball to within inches of the hole. This happened over and over again such that my speed golf lag putts were clearly superior to my deliberate attempts during regular rounds. With tee shots, I'd address the ball, and the club would seemingly rotate independently around my body. My arms would simply hang on for the ride, too tired to interfere with the process. Naturally, the shots would split the fairway and I'd be in full stride before the ball landed. My brother Wally, a crack player with a 3-handicap and three California State Net Amateur Match Play Championships in the lowest handicap flight to his credit, once tried three holes of speed golf on a whim after a full day on the course. Eight minutes later, after an effortless par, birdie, par, he was in the parking lot marveling at the whirlwind. "It's exhilarating!" he said. "The speed of play distracts you from your conscious mind."

The dichotomy of rushing through the most deliberate sport around is enough of a jolt to your nervous system to get you out of your head and into the zone. Try it sometime—but make sure you're first off the tee in the morning or start at twilight on a nearly-empty course, as speed golfers tend to catch up to the groups ahead during their sub-hour rounds! If you are not inclined to head to the golf course, you might want to try a simple exercise offered by New Age author Dan Millman to help you experience instant *satori*: "Take your keys, a piece of fruit or any handy object, and go outside. Throw the object up into the air. Staying relaxed and easy, catch it. Be sure to catch it. Then come back inside, and continue reading.

"Consider the moment the object was in the air," Millman continues. "You weren't thinking of what you'd have for dinner or what you did yesterday. You weren't thinking of anything else, either. You may have been attending to thoughts before you threw it or after you caught it, but during the throw, you were pure attention, reaching out, waiting for the object's descent. In that same moment, your emotions were open, and your body was alert and vitalized. That was a moment of satori."

Accessing a Higher Source of Competitive Energy with the Balanced Approach

A performer who radiates pure joy for competition and competes with a pure motivation and clear conscience can tap into a mysterious, intangible source of energy, clearly evident when you examine the curious phenomenon of home-court advantage. It's common announcer fodder to describe how athletes feed off the energy and vocal support of the home crowd. Obviously, there is no way to measure something like this, except to look at the overwhelming statistics indicating a discernible advantage for home teams in every sport. In a game with highly skilled and focused high school, college, or professional players, there is no logical reason that a home team should have this statistical advantage over a visiting team, regardless of how loud the crowd noise is, but the phenomenon is confirmed true every day.

Tiger's list of accomplishments under pressurized, energized competitive circumstances will convince even the most ardent disbeliever that something supernatural is going on. For pure theater, rivaling Tiger's incredible play-off shot at La Costa is his 1997 hole in one at the loudest, craziest, most unusual golf hole in the world, would be the 162-yard par-3 sixteenth hole at the Tournament Players Championship (TPC) Scottsdale course, host of the Phoenix Open. The numerous TPC courses around the United States are designed with tournament galleries in mind and feature natural amphitheaters and strategic vantage points built into the landscape. The Phoenix Open (now known as the FBR Open . . . I believe the city is still known as Phoenix) proudly claims to draw the largest tournament crowd in the world, with more than five hundred thousand total spectators over the four days. At the sixteenth hole, massive bleachers along with natural grass mounds run the entire length of the hole so that some twenty thousand spectators can observe the action.

This is no ordinary gallery. College kids come in droves and transform the sixteenth from a golf tournament into a football game. Alcohol flows freely as do loud mouths. Forget about keeping quiet per golf gallery tradition; golfers must endure heckling for poor shots and even debris peltings. Brendan McEvoy's colorful article about the sixteenth explains that "hijinks push the envelope and the course goes from fan-friendly to pro-inhospitable. During preshot routines, the chattiness resembled sounds heard outside of a restaurant kitchen—muffled voices and occasional clangs, laughs and barks. The nanosecond each player made contact, half the fans screamed, 'Get in the hole!' If the ball hit the green, the crowd applauded. If it missed the green or was more than 25 feet from the hole, they booed." McEvoy described the typical fan as interested in "booze, babe watching (few tournaments can challenge in this category), and betting [on which player of each group will hit closer to the hole]" and interviewed one, who admitted to not following golf: "We always come for the party. I got tickets from a friend who works with one of these corporations and I heard 16 was the party hole." Numerous pros offered colorful comments in the article. "I felt like I was in the movie, Gladiator," Bo Van Pelt said. "When you walk off 15 green to 16 tee," according to Hank Kuehne, "there's definitely electricity in the air. I love it. Wouldn't want to do it every week, but as far as my first time, I really enjoyed it." And Jeff Slumam remarked, "I now know what a quarterback feels like when calling an audible in an away stadium."

So what does Tiger do on the sixteenth hole during his first Phoenix Open (in 1997)? He hits his ball into a four-inch hole, one and a half football fields away. McEvoy relates, "The crowd roared from the moment that Tiger started his backswing all the way through until he snatched his ball out of the cup." Debris rained in the sky like a ticker-tape parade, and jokesters spilled onto the fairway from behind the ropes to bow on their hands and knees to the king as he walked past them. We can all sit firm and assert that Tiger's hole in one came because his club met the golf ball at precisely the right speed and angle to generate a shot that flew this many yards and bounced this many times into the cup. But if you add up the many incredible clutch performances over Tiger's career, even the straightlaced must wonder if something special is going on. If somehow, the confluence of Tiger's king of the moment mind-set and the incredible intensity of his peak performance arena (and in the case of the sixteenth at TPC Scottsdale, it is literally an arena) adds up to magic.

The odds of a hole in one for a touring professional are 2,500 to 1, but Tiger drains one on the single hole with the most, and the rowdiest, spectators in the world. If Tiger were to head out on a random rainy day to the seventh tee at La Costa and hit six-irons, it would take him perhaps five hundred to a thousand shots to equal the single competitive shot he hit on tournament Sunday in 1997. What about the energy of his explosion onto the PGA Tour in 1996? The tripling of gallery sizes, the Nike-driven marketing phenomenon, the mainstream cultural fascination with the "cablinasian" (Tiger's inventive description of his heritage, a mix of Caucasian, black, "American Indian," and Asian) dismantling the hierarchy and tradition of this country-club sport. Could all this energy have in some mystical way contributed to him shooting an astonishing twenty-one of his first twenty-seven professional golf rounds in the 60s? Even the greatest players of all time, years or decades into their professional careers, have been hard-pressed to produce such a streak of tournament golf, but Tiger did it at the outset of his pro career, under an incredibly intense and stressful microscope.

As Gene Wojciechowski wrote in his 2006 *ESPN Sports* article "Tiger Woods: The Greatest Individual Athlete Ever," "There comes a time when golf greatness morphs into something beyond recognition, something so singular that you have difficulty explaining it. It defies comparison, context and reason. Can you explain Woods?

I can't. I'm not even sure Woods fully understands the ripple effect of his achievements. All I know is that there has never been anyone like him. You tell your children about him, and maybe, if they stick around long enough, they tell theirs."

I believe Tiger's competitive exploits fall in the same category as the amazing, but less spectator-friendly, feats of spiritual adepts who transcend the generally accepted laws of nature and human physical limitations. For example, there have been documented cases of yogis practicing *svadhyaya* (sustained self-study and contemplation) who can manipulate "involuntary" body functions. Most notable was Swami Rama, who in 1960 was one of the first adepts to be studied by Western scientists at the Menninger Clinic in Kansas. His feats included stopping his heart for seventeen seconds and inducing a ten-degree Celsius difference of temperature between his left and his right arms—alternatively red sweaty hot and white clammy cold. Among the astonishing feats of Greek runner Yiannis Kouros was completing a thousand-mile ultramarathon footrace, running around the clock for ten days. The late Swedish mountaineer Goran Kopp rode his bicycle seven thousand miles from Stockholm, Sweden, to Mount Everest, climbed Everest solo without oxygen or a support team (turning back an hour from the summit on his first attempt due to weather and then succeeding on a later attempt), then up and pedaled back to Sweden from Nepal. Back in mainstream America, at the 1978 World Series, Hall of Famer Reggie Jackson of the New York Yankees hit the very first pitch he was thrown out of the park for a home run—three consecutive times at bat! The *Guinness Book of World Records* is full of many more improbable feats where human limits were somehow discarded in favor of unexplainable will and energy.

Using Your Own Crowd Energy

You may never be at the vortex of attention and energy of millions like Tiger nor feel like running a thousand loops around Flushing

Meadows Park in New York City like Kouros. However, you have more than likely experienced this phenomenon in other ways—maybe that time when you were exhausted but dragged yourself to a great party and discovered a new reserve of energy. This energy is floating around, ignored by most but up for grabs if you can be focused, playful, fearless, process oriented, and open minded in your pursuit of peak performance. Some say that the subconscious cannot discern between dreams and reality, so go ahead and envision yourself on the final hole of the U.S. Open, battling Tiger for the championship. If you think this is fun-and-games kid stuff that has no relevance to real-life peak performance, consider this comment from Tiger on "60 Minutes": "My favorite time is going out in the evenings and drop five balls and pretend I'm playing Jack Nicklaus, Arnold Palmer, Ben Hogan, whoever. Throw four to five balls down, pretend I'm playing for the U.S. Open; I pick a venue—I still do that to this day, and I always will."

Motivational guru Tony Robbins says, "There is a powerful, driving force inside every human being that, once unleashed, can make any vision, dream or desire a reality. Create a vision and never let the environment, other people's beliefs, or the limits of what has been done in the past shape your decisions. Ignore conventional wisdom. Even in the face of doubt or controversy, have faith in that vision. Cling to it in the knowledge that you have the right to achieve nothing less than what you want for your life. You're in the midst of a war: a battle between the limits of a crowd seeking the surrender of your dreams, and the power of your true vision to create and contribute. It is a fight between those who will tell you what you cannot do, and that part of you that knows—and has always known—that we are more than our environment; and that a dream, backed by an unrelenting will to attain it, is truly a reality with an imminent arrival."

When I drop a Tony bomb on some people, they make like they wanna hurl. I wonder why? As they say, overly strenuous denials arouse suspicion. Maybe your cynicism over a rah-rah guy is part of what's keeping you trapped in something less than what you want for your life. Tony's spiel could be describing the career path of Tiger Woods. Remember the heat Tiger and Earl absorbed for their insouciant confidence when Tiger first hit the Tour? During a rookie-year interview with Curtis Strange, a 1980s-era top pro turned commentator, Tiger uttered his famous belief, "I think I can win every time I tee it up." To which Strange countered, "But second or third on Tour is pretty good." When Tiger agreed but then restated his objective, Strange laughed and said, "You'll learn." During the post-Masters victory mania of 1997, Tiger skipped out on some obligations on account of fatigue—a college golf awards banquet, an invite from President Clinton to meet Jackie Robinson's wife at a baseball game, and, at the last minute, a Tour event—absorbing scathing criticism as a result. Tom Kite weighed in with, "I can't ever remember being tired when I was 20." Peter Jacobson said, "You can't compare Tiger to Nicklaus and Palmer anymore because they never [walked out]." You also can't compare Tiger's world to anything that happened before him, particularly in golf but also for any other individual athlete.

Tiger had to reach deep down inside and preserve his vision in the face of doubt, controversy, and the highly stressful and chaotic circumstances of being yanked out of his Stanford dorm room and becoming the most famous athlete in the world in less than a year. "I was 20 years old when I came out of college, fairly well-known, but only in golf," he told Tom Callahan in *In Search of Tiger*. "Then, one day in Milwaukee, I'm thrown into the arena, into the fire. That's a dramatic change. There's no school for this, you know. I had to learn everything on the go. I'm 20, and all of the eyes are looking at me. Everything I do is nit-picked. That's a tough way to go. I wasn't able to blend in anymore. People recognized me walking down a street or riding in a car. At that age, it's a hard change to grasp. . . . I tried to be a kid while I had a chance to do it. You're only a child one time. You can never have those days back."

Tiger did an admirable job retaining an intense focus and a healthy, balanced perspective amidst massive celebrity and wealth—elements that intrinsically distort focus and perspective. "I don't see any of this as scary or a burden," he said in "The Chosen One," the December 1996 *Sports Illustrated* article. "I see it as fortunate. I've always known where I wanted to go in life. I've never let anything deter me. This is my purpose. *It will unfold.*"

"I'VE ALWAYS KNOWN WHERE I WANTED TO GO IN LIFE. I'VE NEVER LET ANYTHING DETER ME. THIS IS MY PURPOSE. IT WILL UNFOLD."

—Tiger Woods

Hopefully by this time you can discard your fixation and envy toward the lifestyles of the rich and famous and concede that Tiger did indeed have to endure some stressful, exhausting circumstances, massive pressures and demands, and daunting competition to make his dream unfold. Hence, his story has direct relevance and a spiritual connection with your own vision and challenges away from the spotlight. Do you aspire to a new career, to a better work-life balance, or to repairing a frayed relationship with your teenager? You must step up to the first tee like Tiger does, manage the butterflies, and make it happen. If you feel nervous or negative about the challenges you face, get some perspective about your personal drama. The succession of challenges we heap upon ourselves in life are part of a big, long game, as they are for Tiger—no matter how important you or society judge them to be. After all, ordinary folk, brain surgeons, business tycoons, and golf legends will all eventually grow old and die.

Balancing Competitive Intensity with Letting Go

The importance of a big-picture perspective and a balanced life was asserted by Tour pro Dave Berganio. "You have to be a pit bull on the golf course, but when the round is over be able to leave everything behind and laugh about it. It took me a long time to be comfortable with this skill, but I never lost the sense and the importance of being a good person off the golf course." Berganio has the pit bull part nailed, thanks to his rough and unlikely journey to the Tour. "I wasn't supposed to make the PGA Tour. I was born to a 15-year-old mother and grew up on welfare in the housing projects of Pacoima, California. But I persisted and did whatever it took to make it. I never took no for an answer, and I always believed in myself." After a couple years of junior college golf, Berganio joined the powerhouse University of Arizona squad and quickly distinguished himself as one of the nation's top collegiate players. He was an NCAA All-American, Pac-10 Player of the Year, and played in the Walker Cup (amateur version of the Ryder Cup, pitting a team of top Americans against a British Isles team). Over his thirteen-year professional career, he has amassed earnings of more than $2 million on the Nationwide and PGA Tours, including a runner-up finish to Phil Mickelson at the 2002 Bob Hope Chrysler Classic.

Berganio has gained some keen insights from Tiger and other greats about having a balanced perspective. "Jimmy Furyk is a great example of someone who has never changed. I met him when he was a junior [at the University of Arizona] and he was really struggling. He'll tell you—he struggled, struggled, struggled. We only took five players to nationals and he didn't even make the squad. But he carried on with a great attitude. His mind-set never changed.

He has the same 'nice guy' personality today, even though his pockets have gotten pretty damn hefty and he's the U.S. Open champion.

"Tiger's the same," continues Berganio. "I'm not really close to him, and his schedule doesn't oblige him getting close to many other players. He's got his commercial shoots, business ventures, early tee times [Tiger's M.O. for practice rounds and pro-ams, to avoid crowd hassles and get off the course quickly]—it's a business to him. But he always says hi to me, always smiles. He's an icon and will be the greatest player ever—so he certainly doesn't have to smile! But he remembers our Southern California roots and our several practice rounds together and he's always been cool to me. There's always a positive way of putting things, and guys like Tiger, Jimmy, Vijay Singh and Mike Weir are ones who model that. Weir is another one who struggled for a long time in college, but kept a positive mindset. Now when these guys get to the golf course, they're not so friendly anymore! They're not jerks; they don't wish any ill will on their fellow players. It's more like, 'Hey I hope you make birdie . . . and I make eagle!' "

Achieving Emotional Balance

Dan Millman, whose magnum opus *Way of the Peaceful Warrior* and its many sequels have created a cult following of those seeking the balanced, appreciate-the-moment qualities of the self-explanatory Peaceful Warrior, says that emotions come and go like passing clouds and that the ultimate would be to have free-flowing, unobstructed emotions, like a child. "As infants with unobstructed emotional energies, we felt naturally motivated to explore, move, learn, act and discover . . . when we felt angry, sad or afraid, we 'let it flow, and let it go,' quickly and naturally returning to a state of happiness and bliss."

Obviously, few adults can lay claim to living like a blissful child. Our emotional obstructions stem from the complexity of modern life and the disconnection of the mind from the body. Millman argues that all our descriptions of negative emotions "are derived from three primary states: fear, sorrow and anger." When we hold on to these emotions and let them affect our attitude and behavior, it's clear how they can compromise peak performance. Tennis great John McEnroe and his famous temper tantrums were extremely immature and unsportsmanlike, but they enabled him to clear his emotional slate and focus on the moment. After all, during an intense outburst of anger, your mind is totally focused on the present.

When Tiger has an angry emotional outburst during a golf round (which, unlike McEnroe's, are directed inward so they do not harm or offend officials, spectators, or playing partners—except, perhaps, for any prudes in the gallery within earshot), he is revealing his competitive intensity and his quest for perfection on the golf course. The average professional athlete has a pretty strong competitive fire burning, but when someone breaks eight putters over their knee in succession in a hotel room after losing the 1996 Texas Open by two strokes (as Gary Smith related about Tiger in his *Sports Illustrated* article), that's who I want on my team for the member-guest invitational.

Tiger could certainly consider mellowing these outbursts in the interest of role modeling golf decorum. However, attempts at restraint in this area might—as Tom Callahan's anonymous source pondered previously—compromise his unobstructed emotional flow. When asked at the 2006 Target World Challenge about his temper, Tiger said, "I'm competitive and unfortunately sometimes, you know, I let my anger get in the way. It comes out. There's better ways at handling your anger. Sometimes I don't always do that properly, there's no doubt about that. I try [to curb temper] and will always continue to try [as it will continue to be a problem] because I am very competitive and I like to beat people."

Because most of our emotional hang-ups stem from childhood, it's a good time to credit Tida Woods for modeling this unobstructed emotional flow. As Tiger commented during a "60 Minutes" interview with Ed Bradley, "You have no idea how competitive my mom is. My dad's competitive but he's more quiet. My mom's more . . . vivacious. She shows her emotions on her sleeve all the time. You always know where you stand, what she's thinking, what's going on in her head. It's always right there, very apparent. . . . When I was little, she'd watch me compete. You see her on the side [Tiger gesticulates an intense emotional reaction]—living every moment, dying on every shot." Bradley asked Tida if she still dies on every shot. "Right now I just dye my hair often, that's all," she deadpanned—causing Tiger to bury his face in his hands and admit to Bradley with a big smile, "This is exactly the way it's been [all my life]."

TIPS FOR CULTIVATING A BALANCED APPROACH

1. Achieve physical balance. Balance physical effort with rest and relaxation to ensure high motivation levels and general good health and well-being. Understand that stress + rest = adaptation and that all forms of stimulation must be balanced appropriately with downtime. Reject the compulsive approach, realizing that improvement is more spontaneous than linear. Balance the ironman mind-set in competition with a sensitive, intuitive approach for the big picture, including preparing for competition.

2. Strive for spiritual balance. Respect the Eastern philosophy of balancing opposing forces in all areas of life. Create a vision and pursue it adamantly, accessing a higher source of energy (such as Tiger's incredible shots under pressure or you getting an energy boost from pleasant circumstances) and rejecting society's pressure to ignore dreams and spiritual concepts.

3. Achieve competitive balance. Become comfortable competing like a pit bull and then laughing about the battle over refreshments later. Furthermore, never forget the importance of being a good person and how it is inescapably intertwined with being a champion competitor.

4. Achieve emotional balance. With your emotions, let them flow, then let them go—like a small child. Next, immediately refocus on the present with a clean emotional slate—like Tiger does for each and every shot on the golf course. In particular, discard the main negative emotions of fear, sorrow, and anger so they won't inhibit future peak performance. Instead, shine through the petty details of life, and welcome the hurdles, obstacles, and setbacks you face as an opportunity to grow and prosper—and be sure to dye your hair often.

AP Images/Charles Dharapak

6

RAISING A TIGER
STRATEGIES FOR RAISING A WELL-ADJUSTED CHAMPION IN LIFE

asked the question to many golfing friends of mine: "How does Tiger do it? What makes him so special?" Most everyone shot back without hesitation, "Mental toughness," and almost always referenced his dad in the next sentence. Phil Green, a PGA professional from Newcastle, California, elaborated, "Tiger's dad's training was so rigorous that it made his mind like a steel trap. Think of that advantage, if you took your kid out to the golf course every single day from age two and taught him, encouraged him, drilled him and even hazed him"—but also, as David Owen wrote in *The Chosen One*, "built a high floor under his son's self-confidence, repeatedly assuring him that he was special, that he had an otherworldly gift, that he had been chosen for great things. This may be the single most powerful weapon in Tiger's competitive arsenal today: his absolute conviction that he deserves to win every golf tournament that he enters." Green continues, "Tiger's mental advantage would grow and grow to what you see now. Look no further than Sergio Garcia [and the mental weaknesses indicated by his post–British Open comments]. Here's one of the best players in the game, one of Tiger's biggest rivals, but he thinks 'the world is against Sergio.' "

The relative personalities and heritage of Tiger's parents created a balanced upbringing that leveraged the respective strengths and cultural traditions of each parent and gave him valuable exposure to perspective-broadening philosophies and behaviors. While both were obsessively devoted to Tiger, they managed to avoid all the pitfalls of overinvolved, overpressurized parents and delivered a magnificent balance all the way across the board: between discipline and freedom, guidance and independence, parental expectations and freedom of expression.

"THIS MAY BE THE SINGLE MOST POWERFUL WEAPON IN TIGER'S COMPETITIVE ARSENAL TODAY: HIS ABSOLUTE CONVICTION THAT HE DESERVES TO WIN EVERY GOLF TOURNAMENT THAT HE ENTERS."

— David Owen

In one corner we have the paradoxical influences of Earl, the "softie Green Beret," a multifaceted, multiracial (African-American, Chinese, Cherokee, and Caucasian) character who brought parental devotion to a new level. While many snickered at his blowhard proclamations (for example, that his entire life purpose was to raise Tiger to be the world's greatest golfer), we can now look back with great respect for his strong values and congruent actions. He was a great athlete whose resolve was steeled by the pain of racial discrimination (at the University of Kansas, Earl was the first black baseball player in the Big 7—which later became the Big 8 and then the Big 10—and endured the separate motel and restaurant treatment on the road with teammates) but who taught Tiger to rise above it. "You don't turn it [racism] into hatred. You turn it into something positive. So many athletes who reach the top now had things happen to them as children that created hostility, and they bring that hostility with them. But that hostility uses up energy. If you can do it without the chip on the shoulder, it frees up all that energy to create," he told Gary Smith in 1997.

With Earl it seems everything had a silver lining, no matter how preposterous the logic. About splitting with his first wife and spending little time with their three children, Earl said that the experience inspired him to redouble his family devotion on his second chance, with Tida and Tiger. During his steady decline in health at the end of his life (when he battled coronary disease with separate quadruple bypass and triple bypass surgeries, as well as prostate cancer), Earl famously refused to change his ways, including a heavy smoking habit. Instead, he once offered the opinion that his health problems were a way to appreciate the "life is short—seize the day" lesson and to pass this on to Tiger.

Tiger seems to have inherited these rose-colored glasses. He's mentioned how his wildness off the tee in his youth helped develop his outstanding recovery shot skills. When he was single, he appreciated his "focused lifestyle" advantage over Tour players with families. When he became married and later a father, he lauded the benefits of having more balance, stability, and inspiration in his life. It's oppressively hot in Tulsa for the 2007 PGA—but "not as humid as Florida." And so it goes, whatever the topic, life is always good with Tiger.

Earl commented in Gary Smith's "The Chosen One" on how his experience with est (personal growth multiday seminars popular in the 1970s and early '80s) impacted his parenting. "I learned to give . . . Tiger . . . the space to be himself, and not to smother him with dos and don'ts. I took out the authority aspect and turned it into companionship. I made myself vulnerable as a parent. When you have to earn respect from your child, rather than demanding it because it's owed to you as the father, miracles happen."

Earl's soft side was countered by Tida's legendary penchant for discipline and competitiveness. As related in Tom Callahan's *In Search of Tiger*, Earl once introduced Tiger at a golf clinic as "'a young whippersnapper who's never been spanked.' 'He's right,' Tiger said. 'He never had to spank me growing up as a kid. Because Mom beat the hell out of my ass. I've still got the handprints.'"

"WHEN YOU HAVE TO EARN RESPECT FROM YOUR CHILD, RATHER THAN DEMANDING IT BECAUSE IT'S OWED TO YOU AS THE FATHER, MIRACLES HAPPEN."

—Earl Woods

Tiger commented on Tida's Eastern influence in a conversation with Charles Barkley for Barkley's book *Who's Afraid of a Large Black Man?* "A Far Eastern culture, as anyone who has experienced it knows, is very strict. So you have responsibilities. You had to do what you had to do if you were delegated a certain responsibility, and you never did anything to bring dishonor to your family. You can't disrespect anybody who's older than you, because if you do you've disgraced your entire family. That's kind of how I was raised, and from what I've seen it's a different philosophy from other cultures that I've been exposed to in America that are not Asian. If I didn't say 'Yes, sir,' 'Yes, ma'am,' 'Thank you, ma'am,' 'Thank you, sir,' I'd be smacked in a heartbeat, right on my butt. That's just how it was.

Being raised under two different cultures gives my life a dichotomy that I think made me more well rounded earlier," concluded Tiger.

Pure Motivation + Natural Potential = the Winning Formula for Creating a Champion

One of Earl's greatest legacies was his calculated effort to emphasize a love for the process over the usual model of parental pressure to deliver results. Earl's guidance allowed Tiger's natural talent to develop without interference from negative influences, such as a coach or parent forcing improvement to happen unnaturally. As a junior golfer in Los Angeles, I had the pleasure of playing with a remarkable talent, a kid a few years younger than me who placed highly at Junior World as a preteen. He was fearless on the golf course and immune to pressure, and he attacked every shot with great joy and focus. He lived across the street from the course and played all day long, usually at least thirty-six holes. Once we played sixty holes in a single day, all on foot. He had all the tools and environmental advantages to ascend to the top level, but by age sixteen he'd grown more interested in girls and drugs than trophy mugs.

All kinds of unhealthy influences and distractions can derail innocent kids in the progress toward their dreams. Unfortunately, flawed parenting techniques and values seem to be high in the rankings. Sure, all parents want "what's best for their kids," but that ideal is often twisted to mean wanting them to excel in something that the parents can be proud of. Personal achievement is certainly important, but unless motivations are pure, the value is severely compromised. It's great to support, encourage, and facilitate your kid's pursuit of excellence in sports, school, music, art, or any other endeavor. But there is a line that must not be crossed. A child who connects her achievements with making her parents proud or to her own self-worth is likely to eventually suffer an assortment of negative consequences.

Po Bronson's provocative February 2007 *New York Times* article titled "How Not to Talk to Your Kids—The Inverse Power of Praise," detailed how the parental norm of praising a child's intelligence (Bronson references a Columbia University survey that indicates 85 percent of Americans believe it's important to do this) probably causes more harm than good. Stanford University researcher Carol Dweck's work in this area suggests that kids praised for their intelligence will undervalue the importance of effort and withdraw from new intellectual challenges in order to avoid embarrassment and failure. In contrast, those praised for their efforts are unburdened by the aforementioned psychological baggage and eagerly tackle difficult challenges. "Emphasizing effort gives children a variable that they can control. They come to see themselves as in control of their success. Emphasizing natural intelligence takes it out of the child's control, and it provides no good recipe for responding to a failure," observes Dweck in Bronson's article.

We've read David Owen's pointed observation that Earl built "a high floor under his son's self-confidence" and told Tiger he was the chosen one and so forth; it would be useful to merge these two seemingly contradictory concepts to develop a winning strategy. Clearly, behind Earl's hot air was an evolved perspective on competition and parenting. He believed that Tiger was chosen to give back and be an ambassador for golf more so than to be the leading money winner.

Kids who are smart or athletically skilled figure this out very quickly on their own. As Tiger accumulated his competitive honors and media attention, including his Junior World at the ages of eight, nine, twelve, and thirteen, he didn't have to stretch his imagination to realize that he was a special talent. In schoolrooms and playgrounds across the globe, the highest achievers ascend naturally to the top of the pecking order regardless of adults' efforts to equalize things or downplay natural human competitiveness. The logical conclusion for a parent would be that it's unnecessary, and potentially harmful, to praise natural ability. Instead, one should focus on praising effort and behavior. Furthermore, Bronson's article cites testimony from experts that praise should be sincere and specific because children are skilled at detecting and discounting disingenuous praise.

The important thing is for kids to enjoy the experience of their lives and for parents to help them achieve what my wife calls their *natural potential*. If your kid is destined to be a professional athlete, an Ivy League student, an Oscar-winning actor, or a political leader, this path will run its course with your support. If you pay attention, you will notice signs along the way and respond appropriately, nurturing the child's dream as expressed by her own words and actions, at her own pace.

Maybe instead you will discover that your child has ordinary intelligence, athletic skills, or ambitions. Perhaps this is a gift that will allow him to develop a strong capacity for joy and inspiring others. Who do you think has a greater positive impact on the game of golf and on the planet: a touring pro ranked thirty-ninth on the money list, jetting the globe in pursuit of personal glory and wealth, or the head of the junior golf program at a public course in Anytown, U.S.A.—someone who wasn't good enough to make it on Tour, who oversees the development of hundreds of young players every year? All other things being equal, if Tiger were a world-class klutz who couldn't break 90, he might still be doing great things—caring and sharing in some way outside of the spotlight—thanks to the values that were imparted during his upbringing.

Parents whose common sense is drowned out by attachment to their kids' results perpetuate a negative, superficial, and perilous approach to peak performance. The risk of unhappiness and alienation is high, because your kid gets the sense that love and happiness are conditional. Sure, many kids come shining through in this superficial environment—pulling straight As, landing athletic scholarships, making good coin climbing the corporate ladder, marrying the "right" person, and generally meeting society's expectations so their parents can serve up good cocktail party chatter ("My daughter is a ___. She's married to a ___."). But when you cut through all that fluff and start talking about deep stuff such as family legacy, that's when you have to swallow hard and ponder what the heck you are doing in your privileged role as a parent. The world has enough lemmings and empty souls chasing dollars and acceptance, battling others for energy, and acting out control dramas stemming from childhood emotional wounds. If you pay attention only to your own signs and ego demands, and project your dreams into your children's lives, you are quite likely going to suffer disappointment, distress, and a permanently fractured relationship with your child. Forcing, criticizing, and pushing children to achieve is impure, ill advised, and ineffective by any reasonable definition of success, which must include intangibles such as happiness and enjoyment of the process.

"ONE OF THE THINGS THAT MY PARENTS HAVE TAUGHT ME IS NEVER LISTEN TO OTHER PEOPLE'S EXPECTATIONS. YOU SHOULD LIVE YOUR OWN LIFE AND LIVE UP TO YOUR OWN EXPECTATIONS."

—Tiger Woods

As the king or queen of the universe in the eyes of your children, you have the power to create a different reality for them. You can help them become emotionally resilient, focused, playful, balanced individuals who answer to the highest standards of all—the pursuit of their own dreams. As Tiger once told a golf clinic audience, "One of the things that my parents have taught me is never listen to other people's expectations. You should live your own life and live up to your own expectations, and those are the only things I really care about it. . . . My dad has always taught me these words: care and share. That's why we put on clinics. The only thing I can do is try to give back. If it works, it works."

You might be thinking, "Come on, every kid needs a little nudge here and there. My kid would never do his homework if I didn't push him. And if he doesn't do his homework, he won't get good grades, won't get accepted to a good school, won't land a good job," blah, blah, blah. Sure, kids need to be presented with firm rules and limits to play the game of life and be inspired to realize their potential. School is mandatory, but it offers only a narrow sliver of the broadly defined education that your child deserves. Sports are an extremely valuable arena to build character and learn life lessons, if your kid likes sports. Ceramics classes also offer character development and life lessons to those inclined.

Lindsay Hyatt-Barr was a 1999 valedictorian at Placer High School in Auburn, California, and one of the greatest high school track-and-field athletes in the history of California: a three-time national champion and four-time state champion at eight hundred meters (the only middle distance runner to accomplish the quadruple in the eighty-nine-year history of the state meet). She later won two NCAA titles, running for Stanford and the University of Tennessee. Hyatt-Barr explains that her journey was more one of destiny than of unreasonable discipline or unhealthy external pressure. "I studied because I loved learning, inspired by my parents who are both educators. I ran because I loved the competition. Winning was secondary to my desire to simply compete and challenge myself. I definitely was blessed to experience academics and athletics without pressure from my parents, coaches or even the community. Unfortunately, I see so many pushy parents down in this environment [Lindsay graduated from and now works in External Relations at Stanford University], it's really frightening. I've seen athletes become physically ill before races because of nervousness and external pressures. I can't even imagine; the competition was my favorite part! It's critical for all those involved in youth sports, and even academic achievement to get some perspective that 'more is better,' and 'push your kids until they don't like it anymore' does not work," concluded Hyatt-Barr.

In an ironic twist on the "education is everything" maxim spouted by everyone, Linda Armstrong Kelly (Lance Armstrong's mom) took a more enlightened and pragmatic view. In our conversations and in her revealing book, *No Mountain High Enough*, she related how Lance struggled in high school with authority figures, regimented curriculum, and balancing the time and travel demands of his burgeoning career as a world-class athlete. After banging heads for some time with her son, she finally had the epiphany that it was *her* dream, not Lance's, for him to get a college education—a dream that was becoming ever more unrealistic as time passed. (Lance was booted out of his Plano, Texas, high school by an enlightened principal for missing too many classes, goofing off training for the Olympics with the national junior cycling team in Colorado.) Kelly resolved to set aside her dream and instead redouble her efforts to support Lance in the pursuit of his dream of becoming a champion athlete.

Help Your Child Become an Avid Reader!

Yes, there is only one Lance Armstrong (and there is only one Tiger Woods), and the next kid who blows off school to race his bike will probably be looking at a career path involving a lot of grease—at the repair station of the local bike shop. Wouldn't it be better to get the kid focused on studies and thereby unlock a future of greater potential? Perhaps not, according to Wayne Lumpkin, a high school dropout whose career has involved plenty of bicycle grease. "I hear this 'There's only one Lance' line of reasoning all the time, and I take strong exception to it," argues Lumpkin. "I believe it provides an excuse not to try. When I was young, the concept of American Dream was still emphasized; the idea that you have the opportunity to pursue whatever your heart desires—to become president, an astronaut, or whatever. Now it seems like we quench the spirit of kids when we say, 'don't do it'—using the argument that only a few can make it as professional football, golf, or tennis players."

Richard Motzkin is a Los Angeles–based sports attorney who has become America's leading soccer agent. The firm Motzkin founded, SportsNet, LLC (acquired in 2006 by Wasserman Media Group, LLC), represents stars such as Freddy Adu, Landon Donovan, and Alexi Lalas. Growing up in Los Angeles, Motzkin was the quintessential sports-obsessed youth. He starred on his high school basketball team despite being undersized but was never destined to suit up at the next level. Instead, Motzkin went to law school and continued to pursue his dream, taking numerous sporting forks in the road and refusing to be daunted by the long odds leading to one of the coolest lawyer jobs imaginable.

"Like many young people, sports helped define my character, work ethic, and passion for competition," explains Motzkin. "My career choices have involved tremendous risk and uncertainty in comparison to the traditional and secure route of the corporate lawyer. It was my athletic passion and competitive experience that emboldened me to take these risks and create the career of my dreams. Furthermore, I believe my greatest strength in serving athletes is that I am like-minded: we have to balance being fearless and aggressive with being honorable and sportsmanlike to be most effective," he concludes.

The highlight of Wayne Lumpkin's entrepreneurial journey was designing revolutionary braking systems for mountain bikes. In an industry dominated by giant multinational corporations with large staffs of skilled engineers, Lumpkin—operating with a small support team in Englewood, Colorado—improbably built his Avid

Brakes firm into the world's market leader in hydraulic and mechanical disc brake design and manufacturing. Avid was purchased by a larger firm in 2004, providing Lumpkin with "a liquidity event" that allowed him to reflect insightfully on his journey away from the beaten path:

> I think many elders fail to recognize that kids often have their dream at a really young age. America was founded by people who were not risk averse; they left everything and risked the ultimate in venturing beyond the horizon. I believe that genetic component is still prevalent here. However, our adventurous spirit is suffering from the excessive focus on amassing the proper credentials through formal education.
>
> I've run into many cases, including my own employees, of people who had prestigious advanced degrees but could not think their way out of a wet paper bag. Many highly educated people I've encountered are closed minded—unable to simply organize their minds and pursue the right answer. It's an amazing oxymoron, but it's clearly evident when you examine the product butchery and incompetence prevalent in the marketplace. With our No Child Left Behind mentality, we forget that education is ultimately something you do for yourself; you can be presented with the material, but it is you alone who absorb and process the information.
>
> Many autodidacts [people who learn for themselves] are in positions of leadership and innovation in today's economy. In my case, I took over control of my education at the age of seven. I stopped participating in classroom activities, did the minimum to avoid severe penalty, and just read for myself, and educated myself, in the school library. The classroom was so rudimentary and banal that I simply was incapable of submitting to authority and carrying on. High school was such a waste of time that I dropped out, took my GED test, and moved on.

Lumpkin credits some of his success to the profound education he received via his immersion into the world of . . . professional slot car racing. "Yes, it was a fad," Lumpkin explains, "but it was a very competitive scene [requiring both superior car design and driving skills] that taught me the importance of CANEI—Constant And Never-Ending Improvement. This philosophy became the foundation of my career in the mountain bike component industry."

The Gift of the HAWK

Tiger Woods echoed Hyatt-Barr's "fun first" message during an Asian TV interview in 2003. "One of the things my dad kept instilling in me was the joy of the game. He made it fun for me. A lot of the times I see a lot of the kids, they don't enjoy being out there and that's a shame, you're supposed to enjoy the game, it's a game ultimately and the kids go out there and enjoy it while you're doing it. I think that's one of the things I've learned from my father and what I try to instill in all my clinics is, yes, go out there and give it all you have but more importantly enjoy what you're doing because . . . it is a game for everybody."

Kids have to learn many lessons in their lives. Some valuable lessons are learned when kids persevere under extreme competitive circumstances. Equally valuable lessons can be learned when kids decide and gather the courage to quit something they don't like. When I played in the hundred-pound-limit Pop Warner football league as a seventy-one-pound twelve-year-old, I got my body bashed every which way at practices and played only the obligatory "four plays a game" per league rules, usually at the end of blowouts produced by our 10–1–1 team. I hated practice and hated games more. I wanted to quit in the middle of the season, but after consultation between coach and father about this issue, I stuck it out, buoyed by the "great potential" I had, according to the coach.

The lessons I learned from sticking it out? (1) I was not suited for football and (2) coaches bullshit parents in order to have more warm bodies for their star players to bash in at practice. I didn't need to continue with the season to learn these lessons, though. If my son were to become disenchanted with a sporting experience and have the courage to quit, I would be proud of him. By the way, kids are expert at observing the boundaries between what's fun and what's not; all you have to do is sit back and empower their voice. Life is not something to endure; it's something to enjoy. And sports, of all things, are a "game for everybody."

Granted, the nuances of what to do in every parental situation are an awesome challenge. First you must relax and focus your priorities on something other than social pressures and superficial goals. Recently, a friend related how she fielded an inquiry from another parent as to whether her child was participating in the GATE (Gifted and Talented Education) program at their local school. Upon answering no, she received the sympathetic (or perhaps we should leave off the word's prefix) response of, "Well, I'm sure she'll be all right." Indeed she will, particularly if she enjoys school and childhood via participation in the HAWK (Happy and Well-Adjusted Kid) program. With a relaxed and evolved perspective, you will discover the appropriate parental response to deliver at every fork in the road. Watch your kid engaging in unstructured play, and you'll understand the value and importance of what Jane Healy calls "original thinking and reasoning"—letting kids explore and discover what turns them on the most—instead of heaping expectations, steady critique, and regimented instruction on them. Pursuing the latter strategy can produce a vacuous high achiever, seemingly an oxymoron until you've seen them in action: consumers with no conscience, career climbers with no "life," or self-absorbed "winners" who truly believe that the world is their oyster—free from rules and oblivious to the moral implications of their behavior.

Hopefully, gaining an understanding of natural potential and pure motivation will help you relax and enjoy the experience of your kid growing up. With a supportive, nonpressurized HAWK program approach, maybe the switchboard can light up for more kids in more areas. Then we can all realize the highest expression of our talents as parents and kids.

Supporting and Nurturing Your Kid's Peak Performance

The simple object of the game and the complex, colorful terminology generate countless golf metaphors and analogies. They range from the cultural mainstays such as "par for the course" to the lowbrow dirty joke fodder of stiff shafts and clean balls. The relationship between player and caddie offers a great example for parenting. A great caddie helps the player in every way imaginable—shouldering the bag load so the player can focus and conserve energy; offering factual information about the course; engaging in all manner of strategic planning (club selection, shot targets, reading the break on greens); providing moral support, levity, and a calming influence in the face of pressure; and serving as a counselor and motivator. However, caddies are not allowed to hit the ball for players nor bend the rules to give an unfair advantage by, for example, nudging the ball to improve the lie, providing an artificial target on a blind shot, or fudging the numbers on the scorecard.

Notice any parenting analogies yet? Visit a random elementary school open house with science projects on display, and you might encounter college-level work, ostensibly completed by the little third-grade geniuses. In this situation, the caddies are taking shots for the players and should be disqualified. Caddies/parents can fall short in many other ways that are less blatant but still damaging. One of them is simply being committed to the job. After a round on the PGA Tour, players typically head to the range or putting green for more practice. The caddie will retrieve balls, help the player with technique drills, and patiently support the practice session, even after a long, tiring day carrying a forty-pound bag for five miles in the hot sun. The caddie who says, "I'm too tired, I don't feel like it," has breached his duty and will be quickly replaced by a more committed candidate. Similarly, the parent who works too hard and doesn't have time or energy to play with kids at the end of a long day is falling short.

Another error is to try and force a player to produce more than she's capable of producing, based on age, interest, and ability level. After some rounds, the player is too exhausted to benefit from additional practice and calls it a day. It is never the caddie who initiates or coaxes a player into doing something he doesn't want to do. This concept might be a stretch for parents to embrace, but particularly in sports, I believe that kids should have the decisive voice for where, when, and how much to do—as Wayne Gretzky reminds us about the desire to practice.

This falls in line with the ultimate parenting goal: to support and facilitate the realization of your child's natural potential. There is the often-told story of a daily ritual Tiger and Earl Woods engaged in when Tiger was young. As Tiger relates in the foreword of Earl Woods's *Training a Tiger*, "I would call Pop at work to ask if I could practice with him. He would always pause for a second or two— keeping me in suspense—but he always said yes. In his own way he was teaching me initiative . . . whether I practiced or played was always my idea . . . his role—as well as my mother's—was one of support and guidance, not interference, well-meaning or otherwise." If this phone game had gone the opposite direction (Earl begging Tiger to play with him daily), there's a fair chance that Tiger Woods would be another (yes, there are many) "Remember him?" name from the Southern California junior golf circuit instead of the greatest player of all time.

Would this "kids' voice first" approach apply to academics, chores, and other life responsibilities? The issue bears some serious consideration in today's cultural norm of helicopter parenting. Once upon a time, curiosity for learning carried great value, and high

GPAs were an enjoyable by-product of a supporting, positive learning environment. Today, as our schools mirror the dog-eat-dog business world, "Get the grades no matter what" has become the new mantra. I'll assert that if a kid is tired (only 20 percent of American teens get the recommended nine hours of sleep per night), frustrated, and feeling negativity toward homework or school assignments, a new strategy needs to be implemented in favor of bulldozing ahead. Parenting books mention that kids in the developmental years have difficulty communicating their exact moods and feelings, so you must carefully interpret their casual comments for deeper meaning. If your kid says, "Maybe later," upon an invitation to the driving range, it could quite likely mean no, period. If a kid says, "I'm thirsty," while playing soccer at the park, it might mean, "I want to quit right now."

Sometimes the caddie needs to step up, grab the club out of the player's hand, and say, "Let's take a break, relax, and have a healthy snack," or, on the flip side, "I understand you are tired, but you still have to get up, go to school, and do the best you can today." The natural potential concept dictates that your child has a destiny that cannot be altered by turning up the intensity dial or hitting shots for her now and then when hazards are encountered. Your kid may not want to play golf every single day after school nor show the freakish genetic ability of a Tiger Woods, breaking par before he was a teenager. You have to be careful not to cross that line of pushing a kid beyond her natural ability, progression rate, and interest level. If respecting your kid's voice and the importance of a healthy, balanced lifestyle means opting out of the traveling competitive soccer team or dropping some AP classes off the high school schedule, this is a fair trade. If making these choices jeopardizes a chance at an athletic scholarship or admission to an Ivy League school, so be it. Being a champion is no guarantee of happiness. Witness the many tragic stories of young athletes (or even scholars) burning out for a reminder.

The Success Formula

Daniel Coyle's 2007 article "How to Grow a Super Athlete," which appeared in the *New York Times Play Magazine*, discusses the phenomenon of clusters of super athletes in certain geographical locations. He focuses on the Spartak Tennis Club in Moscow, which has generated an amazing eight year-end top-twenty world-ranked women from 2004 to 2006. Coyle's story pays particular attention to the scientific aspect of developing super athletic ability, with a complex discussion of how myelin wraps around nerve fibers to ingrain repetitive athletic movements into the nervous system.

Coyle mentions the work of peak performance expert K. Anders Erickson of Sweden, author of *The Cambridge Handbook of Expertise and Expert Performance*. "Erickson argues that every talent is a result of a single process: deliberate practice. 'Engaging in practice activity—typically designed by teachers—with full concentration on improving some aspect of their performance' . . . working on technique, seeking constant critical feedback and focusing ruthlessly on improving your weaknesses."

Coyle's article continues, " 'It feels like you're constantly stretching yourself into an uncomfortable area beyond what you can quite do,' Erickson said. It's hard to sustain deliberate practice for long periods of time, which may help explain why players like Jimmy Connors succeeded with seemingly paltry amounts of practice while their competitors were hitting thousands of balls each day. As the tennis commentator Mary Carillo told me, 'He barely practiced an hour a day, but it was the most intense hour of your life.' "

Coyle sums up the success formula with the following list of requirements to build a champion athlete. See if you notice any familiarity with Tiger's story: driven parents; an early start; powerful, consistent coaches; and cultural toughness. When we discuss the lovey-dovey aspects of Earl and Tida's parenting, let's not forget the value of discipline, structure, high expectations, and minimal tolerance for straying from these expectations. Tiger was not allowed out of the house for golf until his homework was done and his room was clean. Earl had zero tolerance for poor sportsmanship or a sloppy approach and offers some choice anecdotes on the topic in Tom Callahan's *In Search of Tiger*. Once when Tiger was "only about five," the family jumped in the car to head off to a tournament, but Tiger had left his clubs behind in the house. Earl secretly stashed the clubs in the car, and they drove to the tournament. He let Tiger stew in the parking lot for a few minutes and then produced the clubs just before the tears started. Lesson learned. "He never left anything behind ever again," said Earl. On another occasion, Tiger was playing in a tournament on his birthday in Miami. "On the first tee, all of the other players sang Happy Birthday to him. His chest was inflated way out. But he threw away a lead and got down on himself and blew the tournament in a funk. I unloaded [in an empty room] when everyone stopped afterward at a restaurant. . . . Who do you think you are? How dare you not try your best? You embarrassed yourself and you shamed me." I wonder if Sergio Garcia would be spouting his conspiracy theories as an adult had a parental influence set him straight way back when?

It's clear that the lesson has stuck with Tiger and will continue to stick. At the 2005 Byron Nelson Classic, Tiger missed his first cut in seven years, which amounted to 142 tournaments, the longest no-cut streak in PGA Tour history. Swedish professional Jesper Parnevik said about Tiger's streak, "It's probably more impressive than all the tournaments he's won. . . . He probably has the toughest heart of anyone who ever played this game. That record will never be broken again." At the postround press conference, Tiger discussed his difficult round and the implications of the no-cut streak. "I struggled warming up and it just didn't quite happen today. It was a very frustrating round because I couldn't quite find where I needed to put the club in the right position to actually make a golf swing. . . . So I was just trying to fly by the night and kind of bandage my way through the finish, but I just didn't quite have it today."

About his ability to grind it out and make cuts even when his swing deserts him, he said, "I think this is more intestinal fortitude than anything else. Days when you just don't have it, you don't mail it in, you don't pack it in, you give it everything you've got. You grind it out. I don't care what kind of game you have, you somehow try to find a way to get it done. You've seen me do it over the years. I should have missed many cuts by now, but you just somehow figure out a way. That's part of my attitude and belief—that you should always have the switch on. You can't turn it on and off."

"DAYS WHEN YOU JUST DON'T HAVE IT, YOU DON'T MAIL IT IN, YOU DON'T PACK IT IN, YOU GIVE IT EVERYTHING YOU'VE GOT. YOU GRIND IT OUT. I DON'T CARE WHAT KIND OF GAME YOU HAVE, YOU SOMEHOW TRY TO FIND A WAY TO GET IT DONE."

—Tiger Woods

Notice that Earl and Tida's expectations and discipline were focused on character development rather than on results. When Tiger was at the top of the world in 2000, crushing everything in his path and gathering the trophies from all four Majors concurrently, Earl told Rick Reilly that "his humanity and compassion need work." No doubt Tiger will implement the same philosophy with his children, the first of whom, Sam Alexis, he and Elin welcomed to the world in June 2007. Of course, young Sam's peak performance pursuits will be under different parameters than young Tiger scrapping for playing time on Southern California public courses (he says he honed his ball-bouncing skills—memorialized in the Nike commercial—while enduring interminable waits on public courses). When you ponder Greg Norman's quote about leaving an empire for his children's children's children and realize that Sam Alexis will never want for anything her entire life, nor can she realistically dream of ever coming within miles of measuring up to dad's success and fame, will there even be a fire to achieve anything?

In an AP story covering Tiger's press conference about a Tiger Woods [golf course] Design venture in North Carolina, this exchange was related: "Is the new business venture a chance to leave Sam and potential siblings something more than a roomful of trophies? 'No, no, it's not about that,' Woods said emphatically. 'They're going to have to earn their own lives. I will provide an atmosphere in which they will be encouraged to go out there' and explore the world. Should his children fail, Woods said they can always return home and 'we'll love them to death. But they have to carve out their own lives, that's their responsibility. That's the way I was raised.'"

TIPS FOR RAISING A TIGER

1. Nurture your child's pure motivation and natural potential. Resist the temptation to project your dreams or society's regimented expectations upon your child—including the popular idea that achievement in formal education or sports is the end-all route to success and happiness. Instead, encourage and facilitate your child's pursuit of his or her own dreams through the HAWK program. Realistically, your child may not become the next Tiger Woods, but maybe he or she can become the agent for the next superstar. Emphasize fun, appreciation of the process, and the development of honorable character above competitive results.

continued

2. Be a good caddie. You cannot take shots for your child, but you can help her navigate the course of her choice and provide encouragement along the way. Pay close attention to signals from your child about what's fun and what's not and how much is enough. This will avoid burnout and rebellion when your child grows older and gains more freedom. Be sure that you exhibit high energy and motivation levels toward your caddie role, and devote sufficient time and interest to the job. By doing so, you will model to your child that family is more important than anything else.

3. Place high expectations on your child. No, not to produce results, but to give an honest, sportsmanlike, and maximum effort in competition. Direct your praise to effort and behavior, rather than natural ability or results. By emphasizing these high ideals, you will help your child overcome the perils of superficial motivation and attachment of self-esteem to results. Instead, your child will develop the physical, mental, and emotional resilience to become a tough competitor. Show your child a world with strict boundaries for behavior, structure, prioritization, and general lifestyle balance so that he or she has an open road to pursue his or her own competitive potential. Do everything you can to support your child in his or her own journey, but make it clear that your child will have to make his or her own way, regardless of how much wealth, power, and influence you have.

4. Apply the success formula. Give your kid every possible advantage to succeed on his or her own road by combining the previous three tips with the optimum practical approach. This formula could apply to all goals, athletic and otherwise—develop excellent technique through constant expert feedback and by focusing ruthlessly on improving weaknesses. Refrain from overdoing it to avoid fatigue, burnout, and flagging motivation levels. Develop cultural toughness by enforcing your expectations for outstanding effort and character and reducing emphasis on natural ability and winning. (It may seem paradoxical, but the toughest competitor is actually the one who can transcend society's superficial obsession with winning to pursue higher ideals.) Model the concept that pursuing excellence is more fun than chopping away with poor technique, a half-hearted attitude, and self-limiting beliefs and behavior patterns. Convey the maxim that your children must "earn their own lives" and refrain from transposing your own dreams and material wants onto your child's blank slate.

AP Images/Eric Gay

7

CROSSING THE RIVER

Dave Berganio, who had a front-row seat for one of Tiger's twenty-seven consecutive victories after having a third-round lead, provides an all-too-simple explanation for Tiger's extraordinary front-runner record. "We were paired together on the final round of the 1997 Byron Nelson Classic," remembers Berganio. "There was a reported 174,000 people paid attendance that day. Our gallery was ten deep the entire way. If we were on nine, you had to jump to the fourteenth hole to get a good vantage point. Tiger shot 68 and won by two shots. He didn't hit the ball great, but he got the job done. Tiger is going to hit it where he needs to, to make par or birdie. He's just not going to make that mistake and give away the tournament. He's always won at every level, so winning on Tour shouldn't be a big deal."

Tiger echoed this when he discussed his success in the Junior World competitions: "Junior World was where my confidence started—knowing that I could play this game against a high level of players—and from then on I felt like I could complete against the best players anywhere around the world," he said in David Owen's book *The Chosen One*.

You can win at your level, too, which *is* a big deal and will require a difficult journey during which you can evolve into the character of a champion. Consider this journey the crossing of a river filled with obstacles that can hang you up or spit you back to where you started. These obstacles are junk you have accumulated during your time in the rat race: compulsions, control dramas, failures, self-limiting beliefs, fear, sadness, anger, negativity, and apathy. As you leave your familiar, comfortable bank to begin your crossing, you can now view these obstacles in a different light. Instead of being afraid, intimidated, or pulled toward them due to a weak resolve, you can leverage the power of rushing water—representing the ever-changing present moment and the irrelevance of the past or even the future—and flow right past them.

Keep in mind that if you cannot get past these obstacles when you venture out into the viciously competitive world and try to pick up some "Ws"—as Tiger would say—you will become gripped by fear and anxiety at the precise moment when you need to keep a cool head—like Phil Mickelson was when he was one hole away from realizing his childhood dream of winning the U.S. Open. "Be happy now without reason, or you never will be," says Dan Millman. That's a tall order to be sure and might cause a certain percentage of readers to exhale with exasperation, but it's where you need to be when you jump into the river.

When you succeed with your crossing and reach the other bank, you can begin making footprints in the clean, smooth sand—in any direction you like. This doesn't mean you should feign indifference or forget about past tribulations, for this is disingenuous. You can remember them forever—using them to stoke your competitive fire but without carrying the weight of them on your back. Consider the example of how Earl Woods guided Tiger to deal with the racism that Earl endured in his own life and that tainted the tradition of golf before Tiger came along. Instead of bequeathing anger and resentment to his offspring, Earl directed Tiger to let his performances speak for himself (for no words can match the impact of an athlete winning the Masters) and to be proud, but matter of fact, about his mixed-race heritage, thereby steering the attention back to his performances and his character.

Committing to Your Personal Interests

Whoever you are, regardless of what your peak performance endeavors are, you can become a champion in the model of Tiger Woods, experiencing and enjoying the pursuit of peak performance. Instead of being a storyteller ("I'm right because . . ."; "I'm not good enough because . . ."; "The world is unfair because . . ."), you can cross the river, stand tall, and announce, "I've made a commitment to a new way."

WHEN YOU COMMIT TO A PROCESS INSTEAD OF AN END RESULT, THAT'S WHEN YOU CAN EXPERIENCE WHAT IT'S LIKE TO WALK THE PATH OF A CHAMPION.

Making a commitment to a new way means you make a decision, set a goal, and do whatever it takes to succeed. To most of us this means shooting a number, crossing a finish line, closing a deal, graduating from college, losing ten pounds, and the like. These kinds of commitments are fluff compared to a commitment to a way of life. When you commit to a process instead of an end result, that's when you can experience what it's like to walk the path of a champion. It is then that you might find yourself sitting in the clubhouse after your nice day enjoying nature, camaraderie, competition, and the focused pursuit of athletic excellence, and, lo and behold (as Tiger said about his 63 at the 2007 PGA Championship, explaining that his goal was not to shoot a record score but simply to put himself in good position heading into the weekend rounds), the numbers on the scorecard just might show 39 + 39 = 78.

To assist your breakthrough, watch and reflect on Tiger Woods on a deeper level rather than merely gaping at his huge drives and fist-bumping fellow spectators when the putts fall. Appreciate the gift of perspective that he gives routinely—such as the idea that his first professional prize check of $2,544 for sixtieth place in Milwaukee was more meaningful to him at age twenty-one than the $60 million windfall he landed from corporate America. Or when the interviewer at a Buick Invitational promotional event in January 2006 asked, "Tiger, how do you follow up on a year where you win six times, including two majors, and made $10 million for the first time in your career?" and Tiger answered, "I certainly have some things I'd like to work on, putting, chipping, with my swing and bunker play and everything. Basically it's trying to get my backswing level better, a little more consistent, which will help my downswing so I can react on the way down. I just need to touch up on those things and try and get them more refined as the year goes along and put myself in contention more often than I did last year. If I can do that, then obviously from there try and get some Ws."

Next question: "Tiger, can you comment on your segue from ten million clams and big trophies to a level backswing?" Zzzzz, zzzzz. Gee, I wonder why his comments didn't make it on "SportsCenter" that night? I guess it's more interesting to learn about illegal dog-fighting rings, petulant trade demands and contract disputes, positive doping tests, or a football team using videotape to steal opponents' play signals. I wonder why the media will castigate Tiger for skipping a tournament when he is physically and mentally exhausted after winning a major championship? In a ridiculous August 2007 Golf.com article titled "Tiger Comes First," Jim Gorant chastised Tiger for sitting out the first FedEx Cup play-off tournament of four in a row in August–September 2007. Gorant drew unfavorable, logically flawed analogies between Tiger and NFL players (the Super Bowl champs play nineteen games in twenty-one weeks, not counting the "hell of training camp"!) and NASCAR drivers ("if they lose their concentration, they could die," but they still race every week!) and declared, "Given a choice between doing what's good for the Tour, his fellow players, and the sport in general, Woods put his personal interests first."

No shit. Is there anyone in Tiger's world—fellow pros, agents, sponsors, media, fans, the PGA Tour organization, and tournament organizers—who doesn't put their own personal interests first? How do you think Tiger got to be number one? He didn't get there by allowing himself to be manipulated by the ultimate example of cold-hearted, vicious exploitation that is the sale and marketing of the modern professional—and even scholastic—athlete. Shout out to all you old-time NFL football players with titanium joints, measly pensions, and not a single dime of commish from those hot-selling retro jerseys—thanks for the heads-up!

Tiger also didn't get to the top by focusing on winning ten million bucks a year, either. Rather, he got there by focusing on his personal interests—things such as balance, being a role model for youth, having fun, and pursuing "peak" performance in a more literal sense than any other athlete ever. Tiger's quest for balance includes keeping his competitive intensity in check enough to skip tournaments when he is exhausted, thereby exhibiting the most powerful competitive disposition ever seen in the history of sports. "My goal has always been the same: To win every event I enter. . . . If I don't feel that way prior to a tournament, I won't commit," he said about his FedEx Cup play-off withdrawal. When Tiger says, and lives, the philosophy that "golf is what I do; it's not who I am," he models a refreshing alternative to the depressing norm of one-dimensional, high-achieving, soulless, selfish achievers and consumers. Finally, Tiger pursues the ultimate self-interest of having fun ("Basically it's trying to get my backswing level better. . . . There's always stuff to work on. You never, ever arrive. But it sure is fun trying."), helping us remember our most empowering priority, even when the stakes are high.

The Big Picture

Admittedly, mastering the physical, intellectual, and practical skills to be a top competitor is so difficult and compelling that it's easy to become preoccupied in this narrowly focused dimension. Those quiet moments when you might ponder mumbo jumbo about crossing a symbolic river quickly get snuffed by the ring tone of your cell phone, another bucket of practice balls dispensing from the machine for you to whack with your demo driver, other distractions of the entertainment age, and, of course, the need we all have to constantly feed our egos. Consequently, we've distorted and misconstrued competition, character, and winning such that we see spectators picking fights in the stands at high school football games, adults screaming critiques from the sidelines at kids' soccer games, and seemingly decent, honest, educated professionals fudging numbers on quarterly reports to keep the house of cards standing. If you can put points up on the board or money in your shareholders' pockets, all is forgiven and you may continue to storm ahead without regard to the negative impact on society and your own character.

> "I AM WILLING TO FALL, AND I UNDERSTAND THAT IT'S OK TO FALL, BUT I AM GOING TO GET BACK UP. I MAY TAKE A STEP BACK, BUT IN THE END I AM GOING TO TAKE A GIANT LEAP FORWARD."
>
> —Tiger Woods

To possess the character of a champion requires a whole different level of existence. Earl and Tida Woods understood this and worked hard to raise a complete and balanced man, so that Tiger could cope and thrive under the most grand and pressurized competitive environment ever seen in sports. "I have a big-picture outlook," Tiger told David Owen in his *Men's Vogue* article. "I am willing to fall, and I understand that it's OK to fall, but I am going to get back up. I may take a step back, but in the end I am going to take a giant leap forward." The true champion is a fearless competitor who lays everything on the line just for sport, to explore the boundaries of the human spirit like Bannister intimated.

Tennis Lessons from Boris

Tennis legend Boris Becker also extends the gift of his perspective about life in the fast lane. In case you haven't paid attention since he dropped off Wimbledon Centre Court and moved on with his life, Herr Boris has had a bumpy road. The night he lost his final professional match at the 1999 Wimbledon, he had a long argument with his wife, Barbara, and then stormed out for a drink at a Japanese restaurant in London. A drunken encounter with a Russian model in the restaurant's broom closet gathered more significance when he was slapped with a paternity suit months later (DNA tests confirmed him to be the father). This event hastened a nasty, public, and expensive divorce. A couple years later, he and his good name were convicted in Germany of tax evasion—authorities there disagreed with him claiming Monaco as his official residence.

In his autobiography *The Player* (English version title), Becker recounted, with stunning honesty and vulnerability, his struggles even when he was the number one player in the world. His challenges included keeping a healthy, happy perspective despite the isolation and psychological pressures of being an individual sport champion, abusing substances in an attempt to deal with an array of physical ailments and injuries, extensive travel for virtually year-round competition, and frayed business and personal relationships as a consequence of the high-stakes game he played. "Is it a miracle that it turned out like this?" Becker says of his life.

Yes. For some years I've been confused, on the wrong path, pursuing the wrong goals. Fame and fortune had become my priorities. I was ruled from the outside and going the best way about losing myself. It was partly for that reason that I caused the [marriage] break-up and destroyed the beautiful dream world. I have an excessive need to take things to the limits.

In search of the way back to myself, I've crossed a few boundaries. I need to feel alive again. Life, for me, means enduring pain and experiencing joy. Only then am I at one with myself. The last two years have been the toughest of my life, but they have also healed me. The fight for my life and my soul finally brought me back to a point where I have the courage to be honest with myself. Enough of the self-deception. Enough hypocrisy. I've made many mistakes, hoping they'd turn out right. Reality, however, had no room for such vain hopes. . . . So there's no contradiction when I say that the hurt and the pain of the past few years has done me good.

Privacy

Tiger's destiny to be the number one golfer in the world is less important than how he handles his destiny, contributes to making the world a better place, and, by virtue of his fame, inspires others to be peak performers and good citizens. Anything less than that attitude and approach is, as Boris explains, self-deception and hypocrisy. As they say, there are a billion people in China that don't care who wins Wimbledon or the Masters.

The same high ideals are important for you and your comparatively anonymous everyday life and destiny, despite tremendous pressure to think otherwise. Come on—who wouldn't want to trade places with Boris Becker? Winning Wimbledon and plunging into the "beautiful dream world" at age seventeen, banking millions of euros, traveling the globe first-class, having beautiful women come on to you everywhere you turn? OK, perhaps Boris has succeeded in setting you straight with his description of the accoutrements to his fame, but maybe you dream of switching places with, or developing a young successor to, Tiger Woods? If so, you're missing the point. Just like you're missing the point if your inspiration from Tiger consists of purchasing Nike golf balls, driving a Buick with OnStar technology, or surfing the Internet to scan pictures of his hot wife. You cannot buy inspiration, honorable character, or self-satisfaction. You have to "earn your own life," even if you're Tiger's kid. The life of the world's greatest and most famous athlete is not for everyone, and it's plausible that the intensity of Tiger's genius and passion comes bundled with torment and loneliness.

Howard Sounes's book *The Wicked Game* quotes numerous sources dating back to Tiger's youth that characterize him as distant, shy, and inhibited from normal childhood and college life by his obsession. And this was all before he became a prisoner of his fame. Yes, Tiger has a 155-foot yacht beyond what you can imagine in your wildest dreams (leather furniture, white silk walls, a fifty-inch plasma screen TV, an eight-person Jacuzzi, a master suite, and six staterooms to sleep twenty-one in 6,500 square feet of "living space"). But your wildest dream must also ponder the symbolism of such a vessel—a reality that requires Tiger to surround himself with ocean to enjoy some privacy (which, as you may know, happens to be the name of his floating estate).

It's arguable that the regulars at the annual BGA (Bro' Golf Association) Championship have a leg up in the joy department over the average tightly wound touring pro. The BGA players (aging college buddies and those in their extended circle fortunate enough to wangle an esteemed invitation to their annual weekend-destination tournament retreat) laugh and smile from the practice tee to the eighteenth green and on through the nineteenth hole and the evening festivities. They wildly celebrate great shots and light up the air with profanity when they hack. They endure the gripping pressure of high-stakes competition (don't kid yourself—the BGA

Championship is a coveted title akin to the PGA in some circles, however small the circles might be), share lasting memories with longtime friends, explore a new venue in a different state each summer (yep, it's in the bylaws), and enjoy a healthy break from the responsibilities of real life for three days. Beer, chips, cigars, and ninety-six poorly counted strokes can still represent a path to enlightenment if you adopt a healthy perspective. Similarly, a trophy room and millions of dollars can represent a path to broom closets and self-destruction if you adopt an unhealthy one.

The critical takeaway here is to be keenly aware of your destiny and pursue your natural potential, regardless of what income it generates; backlash from parents, peers, or society; or other people trying to steal your energy. As the mountain bike entrepreneur Wayne Lumpkin asserts,

I believe my path was laid out for me, like an illuminated airport runway. It was obvious where I had to go. I was given certain gifts and I used them. It's not that I'm congratulating myself for being great. Rather, I feel like I was merely the steward of these gifts. I feel fortunate that I had the opportunity to respond to this compulsion that I felt to pursue my goals and dreams. Furthermore, I saw this path, this dream, beginning when I was seven years old. I realized then that I had a difficult path ahead but that I had to follow it, and that there was no one who could dissuade me along the way. Whatever stood in my way, I had no choice but to carry on.

Well, I did have another choice: I could have just wilted. And I think that is the saddest thing that you can do—especially to a young person. That's not to say my journey was easy; in fact the intensity of my endeavors and competition were so stressful that it compromised my health; that's one of the main reasons why I decided to get out [sell the business].

It's important to remember that I never, ever did this for money. I think we've been socialized to adopt this "bigger is better" mentality that's attached to a flawed expectation of enjoyment. After all, we are just human beings capable of experiencing all different kinds of pleasure. Who's to say that a five-star vacation to the French Riviera is more enjoyable than heading to your local stream to catch a beautiful trout?

The struggling I engaged in was not to accumulate material wealth. Avid was a labor of love, a launching pad where I could see my inventions realized. I designed my products for the sheer pleasure of making things that are valuable and useful to other people. I absolutely love it when I bump into someone on the trail using Avid Brakes and ask them how they like the product. They don't know who the heck I am, but that doesn't matter—I gain the greatest satisfaction knowing I've affected someone in that way.

All It Takes Is a Little Bit of Effort

It appears that Tiger has avoided the traps that snare people at the top of the food chain for many reasons, one of the most potent being that he has been socialized to pursue a life purpose far more grand and meaningful than his own personal accomplishments. "I'm lucky to have two great parents," he told the audience at a 2005 Tiger Woods golf clinic. "They stressed education and family. Golf was nowhere near a priority. . . . My parents always wanted me to give back. If you're a sixth-grader, you should go back and help the kindergartners. If you're in high school, you should go back down to help out the elementary students. They were always big on giving back and showing other people how it was done and how they could become better. I continued to do this [conduct golf clinics with Earl for inner-city kids, etc.] in college. After I turned pro, I decided to start the foundation as an extension of what I've always been doing."

In Gary Smith's article "The Chosen One," Tiger further asserts this point. "That's why I know I can handle all this, no matter how big it gets. I grew up in the media's eye, but I was taught never to lose sight of where I came from. Athletes aren't as gentlemanly as they used to be. I don't like that change. I like the idea of being a role model. It's an honor. People took the time to help me as a kid, and they impacted my life. I want to do the same for kids."

Tiger wakes up every morning knowing that his daily efforts are inspiring millions to play the game that he loves and that eight thousand kids each year hang out after school at a building he built, getting turned on by learning and pursuing dreams. Do you think Tiger can overcome defeat and disappointment on the golf course and handle the stifling pressure of being Tiger a little better when he has a purpose that is greater than making birdies, filling up his bank accounts, and getting his backswing level? Do you think your teenager might have an easier time navigating those years if he or she were a practicing role model for elementary school kids? Can you reference success stories in your own life, where you had a compelling purpose and boundless energy and the outcome was an afterthought?

It's easy to ignore or forget these big-picture things. After all, look at all the distractions you can buy at the shopping mall and the accolades you can acquire for being mediocre. Bart Knaggs, Lance Armstrong's close friend and coleader of a phenomenal business and charitable empire that's evolved from Lance's competitive success, observes how generally accepted cultural behavior contrasts sharply with the approach of champions such as Lance or Tiger. "For our own selfish reasons, perhaps to deny our own weaknesses and short-comings, we encourage setting limitations on people. We collectively do this in a very insidious manner. This kind of shit sells, because we accept standards that are not demanding."

Knaggs continues, "For example, I'm considered a good father by people in my peer group if I skip a golf game to watch my kids play soccer. In return, let's say my business partner comes home early from a business trip; I'll tell him, 'You're a good dad.' *Are* we good dads? Offering and receiving compliments serve mutual purposes and we feel better about ourselves. We propagate that shit and support it because we are scared to face the brutal self-truth of how hard we actually work, how far we perform from our potential, the small percentage of our lives we are really taking advantage of. People don't want to deal with that. People want to be *placated*! They want to feel OK. They can't admit that they are lazy or untalented or barely scratching the level of what they can accomplish."

We hear the tough talk from the succession of Tiger's challengers on Tour, each claiming they're focused, fearless, and ready to challenge the champ. Bravo—that's the spirit! Then I look at some of their physiques and wince. Professional athletes who can't even bother to push away the plate might want to match stated purpose with behavior if they really want to challenge Tiger and honor themselves. At least Chris DeMarco was honest when he said, "I can't do it, I've got three kids and a family." Now there's an honest, vulnerable, and balanced competitor. DeMarco may not be destined to topple Tiger Woods from the number-one-ranking position, but guess who twice fearlessly battled Tiger head-to-head down the stretch at major championships (the 2005 Masters and 2006 British Open), en route to runner-up finishes?

No doubt many of the deluded tough talkers would love to trade places with family man DeMarco. Similarly, you can reject the momentum toward placation, retreat, and distraction and simply go out there and compete, accepting your limitations and imperfections but nevertheless laying it on the line. "We can always make that choice to retreat," Bart Knaggs continues, "and complain that we're tired, out of shape, work too hard and don't spend enough time at home. I prefer to focus on the fact that I enjoy a very rich life. I require plenty of freshness and stimulation to keep me satisfied and at ease, so I continue to enjoy the pursuit of my goals," concludes Knaggs. The next time you miss the green and land in a sand trap, understand that this impending struggle presents another peak performance opportunity to give meaning and richness to your life. When you are able to reject negativity and possess the peak performance disposition of a champion, you motivate and inspire others around you to do the same.

Tiger continued with his closing statement at the golf clinic. "I enjoy giving back. I enjoy helping others. It puts a smile on my face to have all you guys here, enjoying this beautiful day. But please understand that we're here trying to give back and help others. All it takes is a little bit of effort from each and every one of you to find someone you can help. It doesn't take that long, doesn't take that much effort. If there's any lesson I can pass on to you today, that's it."

"ALL IT TAKES IS A LITTLE BIT OF EFFORT FROM EACH AND EVERY ONE OF YOU TO FIND SOMEONE YOU CAN HELP."

—Tiger Woods

Tiger then proceeded to end the performance by booming a three-hundred-yard drive toward a distant scaffold tower in an attempt to pick off the cameraman perched at the top. Upon only narrowly missing the poor guy, Tiger squealed with delight, excitedly gestured about the ball's flight (exclaiming that it flew "right over his head!"), and fist bumped the clinic emcee. Then he was whisked away from the cheering throng in a golf cart, off to the next endeavor in his busy schedule—but not too busy to give back. Because all it takes is a little bit of effort *and* it's fun! This is how Tiger does it.

RESOURCES

Barrett, Connell. "The Tiger Rules." *Golf Magazine*, April 2006.

Callahan, Tom. *In Search of Tiger: A Journey Through Golf with Tiger Woods.* New York: Three Rivers Press, 2003.

Garrity, John. "Tiger 2.0." *Sports Illustrated*, April 2007, 69–75.

Owen, David. *The Chosen One: Tiger Woods and the Dilemma of Greatness.* New York: Simon and Schuster, 2001.

Smith, Gary. "The Chosen One." *Sports Illustrated*, December 1996.

Sounes, Howard. *The Wicked Game: Arnold Palmer, Jack Nicklaus, Tiger Woods, and the Story of Modern Golf.* New York: Harper Collins, 2004.

Stout, Glen. *Chasing Tiger: The Tiger Woods Reader.* New York: Da Capo Press, 2002.

Woods, Earl, with Fred Mitchell. *Playing Through: Straight Talk on Hard Work, Big Dreams, and Adventures with Tiger.* New York: Harper Collins, 1998.

Woods, Earl, with Pete McDaniel. *Training a Tiger: A Father's Guide to Raising a Winner in Both Golf and Life.* New York: Harper Collins, 1997.

Woods, Tiger. *How I Play Golf.* New York: Warner Books, 2001.

INDEX